C000111804

WHISKY TALES

Happy Birthday Pa

enjoy x x x x

WHISKY TALES

CHARLES MACLEAN

FOREWORD BY ALEXANDER McCALL SMITH

New edition published in the United Kingdom in 2008
by Little Books Ltd, London W11 3QW

10 9 8 7 6 5 4 3 2 1

A CIP catalogue record for this book is available from
the British Library.

ISBN 978 1 906251 18 5

Printed and bound by Scand Book, Sweden

CONTENTS

FOREWORD

What does one need to know about whisky? That it is a heady drink; that the best variety comes from Scotland; that it is the colour of a peaty burn tumbling down a hillside in some Highland glen? Yes: most people know all that. Yet there is far more to this subject, and the more one finds out, the more romantic and intriguing does the story become.

Charles MacLean is a man who knows whisky. I have sat with him in his study in Edinburgh on warm evenings and cold, and tasted with him a small glass of amber liquid. While most of us would be inclined to raise the glass and allow the contents to slip down the throat, he instead noses the dram, thinks, and then noses it again. Then comes a well-chosen description of the olfactory response, sometimes surprising in the metaphor chosen. 'Wet straw,' he might say. Or 'like the interior of an old car: cracked leather and burned rubber'. These surprises are followed by comments on taste and on the provenance of the whisky. One learns how it is made; what its history is; how it fits into the whole colourful story of whisky production.

This book brings together a broad taster of the encyclopaedic knowledge of this towering figure of the whisky world. My own scant knowledge of the subject, almost all learned (imbibed, perhaps) at the feet of Charles MacLean, has been much enhanced by reading it. Of particular interest, I feel, is the picture he develops of how whisky production has changed over the past hundred years, and how these small changes might have altered the character of today's Scotch. So far as I am aware, this aspect of the subject has not been explored before, but far from having a demythologizing effect, the mystery – even romance – of why whisky tastes as it does remains intact.

In the past, whisky has been associated with a certain defiance in the face of the excisemen. Things are different now, in an age of large distilleries and big business, but the essential romance of the subject is still there. There is no better guide to this whole story than Charles MacLean, a man of great conviviality and humour, a man whom I, like so many, am proud to call my friend. This is a very personal book. It is Charlie's book, and his generous voice can be heard in every anecdote within it. Listen.

Alexander McCall Smith

PREFACE

This book is an expanded edition of my *Whisky Miscellany*. Strictly speaking, a miscellany is a mixture of writings on different subjects, or by different authors. I have interpreted the word more broadly as a mix of topics relating to the single subject of Scotch whisky, mingled with some favourite quotations about the same subject. I have tried to mine territories that haven't been delved before, and I have used the opportunity to chase down, fill out or follow up a number of topics that have interested me over the years. I should explain that I have been writing about whisky for twenty-five years, and was first introduced to the subject ten years before that, in the late 1960s.

Looking at the way the book has come together (for I did not start with a plan), I suppose the over-arching question the book sets out to elucidate (not answer) is:'How has whisky changed over the past hundred years, and why?' This is rather a grand and serious subject for a small volume, and this book means neither to be grand nor over-serious. It is a conversation piece, not a pedagogic exposition. If you like, it is a book to dip into from time to time.

In keeping with the general theme, early entries look at how the definition of whisky has evolved, and might continue to evolve; how distilleries have come and gone, and why; who owns what today. Then there is a clutch of essays relating to changes in production which may have affected the flavour of whisky: raw materials, maltings, how pot stills are fired, how the spirit is condensed, how it is matured. Next, I consider some aspects of packaging and marketing, and how they have changed over the years. Finally, there are some thoughts (not always serious) about the enjoyment of whisky. Each entry stands alone, and the book does not have to be read from cover to cover.

For this edition, I have added a handful of essays on further aspects of the production process, and about Welsh Whisky (an interesting tale in itself), as well as a couple of tasting notes that I hope might inspire.

The archival photographs which embellish the book have been supplied by my friend George Gainsborough. George probably has the largest archive of whisky-related pictures in the world; he is also a distinguished natural-history photographer, with nine-teen books to his credit under his nom-de-photo George Bernard – and one South American butterfly to his name!

Sincere thanks are also due to Diageo PLC, and in particular to that company's archivist, Christine Jones, and also to the Public Record Office for allowing us to reproduce the advertisements in their collection.

In summary, like the *Miscellany*, *Whisky Tales* is a rag-bag. But I hope that, as well as being entertaining, it will also be useful to those interested in drinking or collecting Scotch whisky: the world's finest spirit, and Scotland's most generous gift to the world.

Charles MacLean,
Edinburgh

LIST OF COLOUR PLATES

1 Usher's Old Vatted Glenlivet (OVG) was the first branded
  Scotch, introduced in 1853. In the 1870s and 80s the firm
  built the largest maturation warehouses in the world, in
  Edinburgh. The family made a fortune, and the year this
  poster was produced in 1904 they gifted Edinburgh a
  magnificent concert hall, the Usher Hall.

2 The first 'Don't be Vague – Ask for Haig' advertisement
  appeared in the *Illustrated London News*, 10th December
  1932, in a full-page display. It was a resounding success, and
  the slogan was used well into the 1960s. This advertisement
  dates from 1935.

3 Bulloch Lade was a well-known firm of distillers and
  blenders in Glasgow, owner of Caol Ila (Islay), Camlachie
  (Loch Catrine) and Benmore (Campbeltown) Distilleries,
  and a range of 'BL' blends advertised under the theme 'The
  Centre of Attraction'. This advertisement, by John Hassall,
  dates from 1911.

4 'Glencupar' is a brand of blended Scotch, not a distillery. This
  bizarre advertisement, by Fred Simpson dates from 1909. The
  caricatures are of well-known people of the day – as many
  men as women, – with Napoleon thrown in for good measure.

5 This advertisement from 1909 by James Thorpe combines
  several common claims for Scotch – benefits to health, royal
  connections, antiquity, military associations – all inspired by
  the dreadful pun on the brand name 'Bothwell'.

6 J.G. Thomson & Co was incorporated in 1820, although
  Thomsons had been selling wine since 1698. Between 1753
  and 1964 the company occupied The Vaults in Leith, now
  the home of the Scotch Malt Whisky Society. This
  advertisement dates from 1875.

7 'The Father of All Whiskies' (1926). Haig's claimed 1627 as the date they first became involved in Scotch, on account of their ancestor, Robert Haig, being 'rebuked' by the parish council of Throsk for distilling on the Sabbath. He moved to Throsk in 1627.

8 Unusually, this poster is advertising a malt whisky when blends were all the rage. It dates from 1905, and was painted by Edward Smith. Saunders himself was caterer to the House of Commons at the time.

9 Stromness Distillery, also called 'Man O'Hoy', flourished from 1817 to1928. This poster by Edward Halliday and John Ellerton, dates from 1905. Old Orkney is still available, from Gordon & Macphail.

10 Cromac Distillery, Belfast, was owned by Protestants, which may be why the firm spelled 'whisky' the Scotch way, rather than 'whiskey'. It claimed to be founded as early as 1776, and operated until 1930. The poster, by Howard Davie, dates from 1898.

11 Bibulous monks were a common theme in advertising around 1900 – there was (and still is) a brand named 'Ye Whisky of Ye Monks'. This is perhaps a reference to the 'Father' of whisky, Friar John Cor. This poster is from 1905 and by Peter Campbell.

12 More bibulous monks, signifying beatific contentment. This poster by Arthur Clark dates from 1898.

13 Illustrating in an 'Old Master' style was not uncommon around 1900. Tommy Dewar was interested in painting and had a fine collection. This poster, titled 'The Shipwreck', is by Henry Gillard and was printed in 1905.

14 'Cement the Quarrel' is another 'fine art' style of illustration, designed to be collected and framed. This painting depicting a Highlander and Lowlander setting aside their differences over a dram is by George Herbert Jupp and dates from 1905.

15 Robert Thorne & Company of Greenock was a major distilling and blending house in its day; owner of Aberlour and Glen Moray Distilleries. The firm went into liquidation in 1920. This elegant poster by W.H. Waller dates from 1898.

16 This is part of a series sending up the *belle monde* of London in the 1920s. It is by Doris Zinkeisen, a fashionable costume and set designer, and first appeared in *Country Life* in 1927.

17 Tom Brown's 'Striding Man' was created in 1909 and rapidly became the most famous logotype in the world. Sir Alex Walker claimed that the artist had 'copied my grandfather's face and style', although it is unlikely there were any Regency bucks in Kilmarnock!

18 Strathmill Distillery was built in 1891 and quickly bought by W. & A. Gilbey, the London wine and spirits merchant. Unusually, it was sold as a single malt, even in 1907, when this poster was designed by Alfred Pearce, Arthur Buchanan and John Hull.

19 Chester's was a brewery (closed by Whitbread in the 1980s). This poster from 1907, by Charles Lee, implies that their whisky was so good that the staff could not resist tippling it.

20 Is the priest being tempted by the whisky or the barmaid? Will he miss his train? Such subtle tensions have been conjured by Victor Verner in 1904.

WHAT'S IN A NAME?

*'Usquebaugh': a compounded distilled spirit, being
drawn on aromaticks; and the Irish sort is particularly
distinguished for its pleasant, mild flavour.
The Highland sort is somewhat hotter, and by
corruption in Scottish they call it 'whisky'.*

SAMUEL JOHNSON, *DICTIONARY* (LONDON, 1755)

Far be it from me to dispute with 'The Prince of
Dogmatists', but I am afraid Dr Johnson is confusing
his *uisge beathas* with his *usquebaughs*.

Uisge beatha, from which the word 'whisky' derives,
is the Gaelic equivalent of *aqua vitae*: 'the water of
life'. In the eighteenth century, official documents
still referred to spirits by the Latin term, and the
Gin Act of 1736 lists *Aqua Vitae* and *Usquebaugh* as
different spirits. Two years previously, Lord George
Murray had complained to the Duke of Atholl that
'I have not one drop of either *usquba* or *acquavitae*
in the house'.

Twenty years after he had compiled his famous dictionary, Dr Johnson had firsthand experience of whisky with his Scottish friend James Boswell, and was able to expand upon his definition in *A Journey to the Western Isles of Scotland*:

> *The word whisky signifies water, and is applied by way of eminence to strong water, or distilled liquor. The Spirit drunk in the north is drawn from barley; I never tasted it except once for experiment, at the inn in Inveraray, when I had thought it preferable to any English malt Brandy. It was strong, but not pungent, and was free from empyreumatic [burnt, acrid] taste or smell; what was the process I had no opportunity of enquiring, nor do I wish to improve the art of making poison pleasant.*

WHAT IS WHISKY?
Uisge beatha and aqua vitae

'Whisky' derives from the Gaelic *uisge beatha*, 'water of life' (pronounced *Ooshky-bay*), progressively anglicized from *uiskie* (c. 1618) to *whiskie* (1715) to *usky* (1736) and 'whisky' in 1746. Until the late eighteenth century, the term was colloquial; official and unofficial documents referred to it as *aqua vitae* or *aquavite*: Latin for 'water of life' or the Gaelic *uisge beatha*. Even Robert Burns referred to Scotch spirit as *aqua vitae* in *The Author's Earnest Cry and Prayer* (1785):

> *Tell them wha hae the chief direction,*
> *Scotland an' me's in great affliction,*
> *E'er sin' they laid that curst restriction*
>   ON *AQUA-VITAE*

The first written reference to *aqua vitae* is in the instruction given by King James IV in 1494 to Friar John Cor 'to make *aqua vitae* VIII bolls of malt'. Earlier that year, and the year before, the king had been campaigning against the Lord of the Isles on the west coast of Scotland, and it is generally accepted that he encountered *aqua vitae* there, where it will have been known as *uisge beatha*.

So maybe *uisge beatha* is the earlier term? Certainly, the words *uisce* 'water' and *beothu* 'life' are both Old Irish, and thus date from AD 800–1000. The term *aqua vitae* was first applied to whisky in the thirteenth century by the great alchemist Roger Bacon.

> With fongs and dance we celebrate the day,
> And with due honours *ufher* in the May. *Dryden.*
> The Examiner was *ufhered* into the world by a letter, fetting forth the great genius of the author. *Addifon.*
> Oh name for ever fad, for ever dear!
> Still breath'd in fighs, ftill *ufher'd* with a tear. *Pope.*

USQUEBA′UGH. *n. f.* [An Irifh and Erfe word, which fignifies the water of life.] It is a compounded diftilled fpirit, being drawn on aromaticks; and the Irifh fort is particularly diftinguifhed for its pleafant and mild flavour. The Highland fort is fomewhat hotter; and, by corruption, in Scottifh they call it *whifky.*

U′STION. *n. f.* [*uftion*, Fr. *uftus*, Lat.] The act of burning; the ftate of being burned.

USTO′RIOUS. *adj.* [*uftum*, Lat.] Having the quality

Samuel Johnson's definition of 'whisky' – here 'Usquebaugh' – as recorded in his famous Dictionary of 1755

Usquebaugh

A problem arises with the common and early use of *usquebaugh* as a phonetic rendering of *uisge beatha*. It has been claimed that the spirits made in Ireland were the former, and those made in Scotland the latter. Would that it were as simple as this! Martin Martin, himself a Gael and Macleod of Dunvegan's factor (i.e. a land agent), made a tour of the Western Isles in the 1690s. He began his journey in Lewis, where he noted:

> *Their plenty of Corn was such, as disposed the Natives to brew several sorts of Liquors, as common Usquebaugh, another call'd Trestarig, id est, Aqua-vitae, three times distilled, which is strong*

and hot; a third sort is four-times distill'd, and this by the Natives is call'd Usqubaugh-baul, id est Usquebaugh, which at first taste affects all the members of the Body: two spoonfuls of this Last Liquor is a sufficient dose; and if any Man exceed this, it would presently stop his breath, and endanger his Life.

In The Compleat Body of Distilling, published in London in 1725, George Smith gives various recipes for Usquebaugh, all of which describe it as a 'compounded liquor'. A typical example adds mace, cloves, cinnamon, nuts, coriander, cubebs (berries of the Piper cubeba plant), raisins, dates, liquorice, saffron and sugar to a mix of 'rectify'd Malt spirits and Molossus [molasses] spirits'. But when, in 1755, Dr Johnson published his famous Dictionary, he defined usquebaugh as being 'a compounded distilled spirit, being drawn on aromaticks; and the Irish sort is particularly distinguished for its pleasant, mild flavour. The Highland sort is somewhat hotter, and by corruption in Scottish they call it whisky'.

So *uisge beatha* = *usquebaugh* (a compounded spirit, i.e. with herbs and spices added) = whisky? I tremble to contradict the good Doctor, but I do not think so. There is plenty of evidence for herbs and spices, and also berries and other fruits, being added to *aqua vitae* in the fifteenth, sixteenth and seventeenth centuries, for medicinal purposes, or simply to make a coarse spirit palatable. But it seems to me that, at least by the 1750s, the term 'whisky' meant the pure spirit (*uisge beatha* or *aqua vitae*) and *usquebaugh* a compounded liquor.

Whisk(e)y

The final problem is the spelling of 'whisky' and 'whiskey'. As we all know, the latter spelling is now reserved for Irish and American whiskey (although the American brands Maker's Mark and Dickel perversely uses the Scotch spelling), while the former applies to Scotch, Canadian and Japanese. But this is a modern convention. There are many advertisements from the 1900s for both 'Scotch whiskey' and 'Irish whisky', and the Royal Commission on Whiskey 1908-09 includes the 'e' throughout its definitions.

A late seventeenth-century whisky still

The First Legal Definition of Scotch

The Royal Commission supplied the first legal definition of whisky as 'a spirit obtained from a mash of cereal grains saccharified by the diastase of malt' (meaning that starch in the grains had been converted to sugar), and Scotch whisky as 'whiskey so defined, distilled in Scotland, and Irish whiskey, as so defined, distilled in Ireland'. This meant that any kind of grain could be used (wheat, maize, rye, etc – not just malted barley) and that whisky could legitimately be made in any kind of still, not just pot stills.

This did not please the malt-whisky distillers, who used pot stills and argued that the definition should be limited to their product, excluding grain spirit and thus also blended whisky (a mix of malt and grain whiskies). But it was in keeping with popular feeling. As *The Times* put it two years before the Royal Commission sat:

> *If the public want mild whisky [patent-still spirit flavoured with 'high-flavoured whisky from a pot still'] they will get it, even if they should have to relinquish the romantic notion that it is descended from* usquebaugh. *It is rather a droll notion that a liquor which pleases the public is to be put under a ban because it is not made exactly as liquor was made by our rude fore-fathers in an apparatus of unknown antiquity.*

Later Legal Definitions

Scotch whisky is the most tightly defined of all spirits. This prevents whisk(e)y made outside Scotland, or made with any additives (including artificial enzymes to achieve saccharification), being sold as 'Scotch'.

The 1909 definition was tightened only six years later by the Immature Spirits Act of 1915, which required that whisky must be bonded for two years prior to bottling. This was increased to three years in 1916, and has remained part of the definition ever since. One of the reasons for the legislation was that it was believed that drinking young whisky made you 'fighting *fu*' ('full' or slightly drunk in Scots dialect), while mature spirits made you mellow!

The original definition did not cover a blend of Irish and Scotch whiskies, and this was tested in the Scottish courts in 1938, when a Glasgow firm was charged under the Merchandise Marks Acts with wrongly describing 300 bottles of blended whisky as 'Scotch', when they contained one-third Scotch malt and two-thirds Irish grain whiskey. The court of appeal maintained that both malt and grain components must be made in Scotland for the bottle to be labelled 'Scotch whisky'.

Until 1988, amendments to the definition of Scotch whisky – including the provision that all components of blended Scotch whisky must themselves be 'entitled to the description Scotch whisky' – were enshrined in the Finance Acts. The British government saw Scotch merely as a means of raising revenue. That year, Bill Walker, the teetotal MP for East Fife, introduced a private member's bill which became the Scotch Whisky Act of 1988.

The current definition is supplied by this important act (and the orders made under it, which came into effect in June 1990). 'Scotch Whisky' means whisky:

1. which has been produced at a distillery in Scotland from water and malted barley (to which only the whole grains of other cereals may be added) all of which have been:

    a. processed at that distillery into a mash;

    b. converted to a fermentable substrate only by endogenous [not artificial] enzyme systems;

    c. fermented only by the addition of yeast;

2. which has been distilled at an alcoholic strength by volume of less than 94.8 percent [96.4 percent is pure alcohol] so that the distillate has an aroma and taste derived from the raw materials used in, and the method of, its production;

3. which has been matured in an excise warehouse in oak casks of a capacity not exceeding 700 litres, the period of that maturation being not less than three years;

4. which retains the colour, aroma and taste derived from the raw materials used in, and the method of, its production and maturation;

5. to which no substance other than water and spirit caramel has been added.

The act also prohibits the production in Scotland of whisky other than Scotch whisky, as defined.

A later order made under the act in 1990 adds the requirement that, to be sold as 'Scotch', the whisky must not be bottled at less than forty percent alcohol by volume (ABV). The reason for this is that there is a sharp falling off of aroma and flavour if it is bottled below forty percent.

This early twentieth-century Dalmore advertisement responded to the question: 'What is whisky?', thereby capitalizing on the declared official status of Scotch by the British Royal Commission on Whisky, 1909

Recent Developments

The provisions of the 1988 act were incorporated into European Economic Community legislation in 1989, and the Order of 1990, already referred to, tightened this definition. There is still room for further definition.

In 2003, there was a row within the Scotch whisky industry about Cardhu being changed from a single malt (the product of Cardhu Distillery) to a 'pure' malt (the vatted products of two or more distilleries). It was generally agreed that this move was confusing for consumers, especially since the packaging of the pure malt was very similar to that of the single malt.

Such a move is not unprecedented. Tobermory, long labelled 'The Malt Scotch Whisky', was a vatted malt from 1973 to 1993 – not the single product of Tobermory Distillery. During the 1970s, Mill Burn was a 'pure malt', not the product of Millburn Distillery. Longrow, Lochindaal, Glenfyne, Kincaple, Ferintosh, Adelphi, Octomore and many others are or were single-malt whiskies, but they are not the product of the distilleries named on the label, all of which are extinct.

When it comes to blended whiskies, the labelling is even less defined. 'Fine Old', 'Rare Old', 'Choice Old', 'Extra Special', 'Special Reserve', 'Aged', 'Finest', 'Oldest Matured' and so on are terms that need not necessarily bear any relation to the quality or age of the whiskies which make up the blend, although the description 'Liqueur', once common, has now been abandoned by general agreement within the whisky industry (and I believe by EC regulation), except for true 'whisky liqueurs' such as Drambuie, Glayva and Atholl Brose.

UNDERSTANDING THE LABEL

Scotch Whisky – defined by law (see above); the term implies a blended whisky.

Scotch Malt Whisky – defined by law (see above); the term implies a malt whisky.

Scotch Grain Whisky – defined by law (see above); the term implies a grain whisky.

Blended Scotch Whisky – defined by law (see above); the term implies a blended whisky: a mix of Scotch malt and grain whiskies.

Single-Malt Whisky – the product of a single distillery, usually but not necessarily from the distillery named on the label (it may be a brand name).

Single-Grain Whisky – the product of a single distillery, usually but not necessarily from the distillery named on the label (it may be a brand name).

Pure Malt Whisky – a mix of malt whiskies.

Vatted Malt Whisky – the same as a pure malt whisky.

Single Cask Malt/Grain – bottled from an individual cask.

Non-Chill-Filtered Whisky – (may be malt, grain or blended) where the whisky has not been 'polished' on the bottling line by reducing its temperature to close to 0°C and pushing it through a bed of filters in order to maintain its brightness and clarity.

Natural Strength/Cask Strength – not defined by law, but implies that the whisky is bottled 'straight from the cask', without its strength being reduced to the usual 'bottling strength' of 40 per cent or 43 percent ABV. The strength varies from cask to cask, and is usually associated with 'single-cask' bottlings.

Wood-Finished/Double-Matured – where the whisky, usually malt, has been matured in one cask and then re-racked for the final months of maturation into another cask.

Age – if a whisky label bears an age statement, this is the age of the youngest whisky in the vatting or blend.

Glenturret Distillery, Crieff, circa 1887

THE DEIL'S AWA
WI' THE EXCISEMAN

The deil cam fiddlin thro' the town,
And danc'd awa wi' the Exciseman,
And ilka wife cries, 'Auld Mahoun,
I wish you luck o' the prize, man.'

Chorus:
The deil's awa, the deil's awa,
The deil's awa wi' the Exciseman,
He's danced awa, he's danced awa,
He's danced awa wi' the Exciseman.

We'll mak our maut, and we'll brew our drink,
We'll laugh, sing, and rejoice, man,
And mony braw thanks to the meikle black deil,
That danc'd awa wi' the Exciseman.

ROBERT BURNS, 1792

By 1792, Robert Burns had served four years as an exciseman, but his attitude to the service remained ambiguous. Indeed, even while his petition to join the service was being considered, in 1787, he nearly blew his chances by inscribing an anti-Hanoverian poem on a window in Stirling. He was visiting Stirling Castle, and was so dismayed by the condition of James IV's great renaissance palace (recently restored) that he wrote:

… Stewarts once in glory reign'd,
And laws for Scotland's weal ordained…
A race outlandish fills their throne:
An idiot race, to honour lost –
Who know them best despise them most.

Too late he realized that such lines were hardly flattering to a king whose service he hoped to enter. Indeed, excise officers had to swear an oath to defend the king personally against all 'traitorous conspiracies and attempts'. When he returned to Stirling two months later, Burns knocked out the window. But the verse had already been copied and publicly circulated. He felt humiliated and was admonished, but his petition was not barred.

Poet and hopeful exciseman Robert Burns

WHISKY AND WHISKEY

As stated earlier (see page 17), it has become customary for 'whisky' without an 'e' to refer to Scotch, Canadian and Japanese whiskies, while 'whiskey' is reserved for the products of Ireland and America. But this is convention, not law; Maker's Mark (a Bourbon from Kentucky) and George Dickel (a Tennessee whisky) drop the 'e'; Paddy (from Cork) only adopted the 'e' in 1966. So-called whiskies (or whiskeys) – some good, some nasty – are made in dozens of countries around the world, and their makers use one spelling or the other. It matters not.

What does matter is the difference between them. The various kinds of Scotch – malt, grain, blended, vatted, liqueur – have been defined in the previous chapter. Here I want to look at what distinguishes the makes of Ireland, the United States, Canada and Japan: the leading whisk(e)y producers.

Irish Whiskey

Broadly, the definition of Scotch is the same for Irish: i.e. distilled in Ireland from a mash of cereals, matured there in oak casks for at least three years, and bottled at no less than forty percent ABV. Additionally, Irish whiskey comes in five styles.

Irish pot-still whiskey

This is the key difference between Irish and Scotch. Pot-still (usually called 'pure pot-still') whiskey is made from a mix of malted and unmalted barley in pot stills. In the past, other grains (particularly rye, wheat and oats) were also added, making for a heavy, oily style. Typically it was also triple-distilled, which lightened it. There are only three distilleries in Ireland: Midleton (County Cork), Cooley (County Louth) and Bushmills (County Antrim). The first two produce pot-still whiskey; the best-known brands such as Redbreast and Midleton are made at Midleton Distillery.

Irish malt whiskey

Like Scotch malt, this is distilled from a mash of malted barley in pot stills. By the 1880s, it had become customary to dry the malt in closed kilns, so it was not exposed to peat smoke. Traditionally, the whiskey was triple-distilled. All bottled Irish malt whiskey comes from Bushmills and Cooley Distilleries; Midleton has pot stills, but its malt goes for blending. Bushmills Malt was introduced in 1988, Cooley's Tyrconnell Single Malt in 1993 and its Connemara Peated Single Malt in 1996.

Irish grain whiskey

Like Scotch grain whisky, this comes from a mash of maize or wheat, saccharified with a small amount of green malt and is made in a continuous or patent still. None is bottled as a single grain.

Irish whiskey

A blend of Irish malt, grain and pot-still whiskeys. The large Midleton Distillery produces around a dozen different styles of single whiskey under one roof. Blended, these dozen styles make upwards of thirty blended whiskeys, including the market leaders Jameson's, Powers and Paddy.

Irish liqueur whiskey

A mix of Irish spirit and cream, pioneered by Bailey's Irish Cream Liqueur, which was inspired by Irish coffee (itself invented at Shannon Airport in 1952), launched in 1974. Bailey's is the world's best-selling liqueur.

American Whiskey

The secrets of distilling, and the fondness for spirits, were introduced to the Americas by the first European settlers: German and Dutch, as well as English, Irish and Scots. The earliest 'whiskey states' were Pennsylvania and Maryland. After the 'Whiskey Rebellion' of 1794, which was a rebellion against excise tax on distilled liquor, many distillers headed south and west through Virginia to Kentucky and Tennessee.

Most American whiskey is made in hybrid continuous stills,[1] comprising a columnar 'beer still and a pot-still 'doubler': copper stills that increase the strength of the spirit. Like Scotch grain whisky, it must be distilled at less than ninety-five percent ABV (190° US proof) to have 'the taste, aroma and characteristics generally attributed to whiskey'. If distilled at higher strength it becomes 'neutral spirit'. There are three classic styles of American whiskey.

Bourbon

Although Bourbon County, Kentucky, is considered the birth-place of America's most famous whiskey, Bourbon can be made anywhere in the US. Corn (maize) is its principal ingredient (at least fifty-one percent), with between twenty percent and thirty percent of rye or wheat and some malted barley added. The difference between one Bourbon and another is largely down to the 'mash bill' (the proportion of corn to 'small grains') and what small grains are used. If the corn content is more than eighty percent, it becomes 'corn whiskey'. Another element that Bourbon-makers believe makes a difference (unlike Scotch distillers) is the yeast strain. These are carefully guarded and passed down from generation to generation of distillers.

An additional factor that differentiates the process from that of Scotch is the addition of 'backset' or 'sour mash' to the fermenting vessel, and in some cases to the mash tun as well. Backset is a slurry of liquid yeast and spent grains collected from the foot of the first still (called the 'beer still'). It makes up at least twenty-five percent of the volume of the mash – in some cases more – and performs the necessary function of lowering its alkalinity, since Kentucky water is very high in calcium.

Bourbon must be distilled at less than eighty percent ABV (160° US proof) and it must be matured in new, charred, white-oak barrels. There is no minimum period for aging, but it may not be called 'straight' rye unless it has been matured for at least two years, and it must bear an age statement on the label unless it has been in wood for at least four years. The term 'straight' also indicates that the whiskey has not had any neutral spirit added to it (see below), although it may contain Bourbon from more than one distillery.

Leading straight Bourbons include brands such as Jim Beam, Maker's Mark, Wild Turkey, Heaven Hill, Ancient Age, Woodford Reserve, Old Crow and Old Grandad.

Rye whiskey

This was the original American whiskey, but very little is now produced exclusively from rye. It is made and matured in a similar way to Bourbon, except that at least fifty-one percent rye is substituted for corn, the rest of the mash being made up of malted barley and corn. Notable straight ryes are Van Winkle Family Reserve, Old Overholt, Sazerac and Rittenhouse.

Tennessee sour mash

Although 'sour-mashing' is employed in making rye and Bourbon whiskey, the whiskeys of Tennessee use the term as part of their appellation. They are made in the same way as the other two, but the spirit is filtered through a ten-foot-deep bed of charcoal prior to filling into cask, a system known as the 'Lincoln County Process'. The leading brand of Tennessee whiskey (and the best-selling American whiskey) is Jack Daniel's. George Dickel Tennessee whiskeys also sell around the world.

In addition to the three main styles described above, there are two blended styles of American whiskey.

Blended rye or Bourbon

This is a mix of either rye or Bourbon with neutral spirit, in proportions of no less than fifty-one percent to forty-nine percent.

Blended American whiskeys

These are permitted to contain a minimum of only twenty percent straight whiskey, the rest being neutral spirit. They are cheaper to make, and tend to be smoother, blander and lighter-bodied than straight whiskies. Typical blends are Seagram's 7 Crown, Kessler, Kalvert Extra and Imperial.

Canadian Whisky

Canadian whisky is almost all blended,[2] and the key to the blend is invariably rye whisky. Its definition (including that of 'Canadian rye whisky' and 'rye whisky') is not as tight as that for Scotch and American, although it includes the Scottish three-years maturation rule. It states simply that the product must be 'whisky distilled in Canada and possessing the aroma, taste and character generally attributed to Canadian whisky'.

This allows Canadian distillers to use a high proportion of neutral spirit: as much as ninety-seven percent in cheaper blends. It also allows them to produce a baffling range of blending whiskies from their nine distilleries, and typically around twenty will go into a blend. Mash may contain rye, malted rye, barley, malted barley, corn and wheat; fermentation is achieved with different yeasts; distillation takes place in a range of different continuous stills, including both patent, Coffey stills, and American-style hybrid stills, at different strengths; and maturation is done in new or refill casks, ex-brandy as well as ex-Bourbon. Within the definition it is even permissible to add flavourings such as sherry, wine (particularly prune wine) or fruit juices.

For example, Canadian Club uses a triple-distilled corn spirit, fermented with a specific yeast strain, a double-distilled flavouring spirit and a single-distilled spirit made from rye, malted rye and barley. Seagram's Crown Royal is made mainly from corn whisky matured for three years in new wood before being blended with aged rye whisky. Black Velvet combines young rye whisky and blends this with other base spirits prior to four years of maturation.

Japanese Whisky

Japanese whisky is similar in composition to Scotch. The country has a clutch of traditional malt and grain distilleries, of which the most important are Yamazaki, Yoichi, Hakushu, Sendai and Sanraku. The first two are owned by Suntory, which makes around seventy percent of Japan's whisky; the second two by Nikka; the last by Sanraku Ocean. As well as making their own whisky, these companies also import Scotch malt whisky in bulk and blend it with their own malt and grains to produce a large number of blended brands.

Whisky distilling was introduced to Japan by a single

individual: Masataka Taketsuru. Taketsuru came to Scotland in December, 1918, expressly to find out how Scotch was made. He was twenty-five years old and had been trained as a chemist. He served brief apprenticeships at Longmorn, Bo'ness (a grain distillery) and Hazelburn Distillery in Campbeltown, and attended a Glasgow University summer school in chemistry. In 1920, he returned to Japan with a Scottish wife, and was recruited by Shinjiro Torii, the founder of Suntory, who was interested in building a malt whisky distillery at Oh-Yamazaki, near Kyoto.

In the mid-1930s, Taketsuru left Suntory, founded Nikka and established his own malt-whisky distillery at Yoichi on Japan's mountainous northern island of Hokkaido, which has a landscape and climate similar to the Highlands of Scotland. Indeed, he was drawn to the spot by the availability of cold melt-water and an abundance of peat. Until the early 1970s, Yoichi malted its own barley, drying it over peat fires; today, malt is imported from various countries.

Nikka built another malt-whisky distillery in 1969 at Sendai, in the north of the principal island of Honshu, and a grain distillery with Coffey stills at Nishinomiya, near Osaka. The company produces a range of blends, and has recently started to offer Yoichi as a single malt to compete with Yamazaki single malt, which was introduced in the mid-1980s.

---

[1] All except one: Woodford Reserve, from the recently revived Labrot & Graham Distillery, where three pot stills have been installed.

[2] A very small amount of single-malt whisky is offered by Glenora Distillery on Cape Breton Island, Nova Scotia. The distillery, modelled on a Scottish malt distillery, went into production in 1990. Much of its make goes into a blend called Breton's Hand & Seal.

SCOTCH DRINK

O Whisky! Soul o' plays and pranks!
Accept a bardie's gratefu' thanks!
When wanting thee, what tuneless cranks
    Are my poor verses!
Thou comes — they rattle in their ranks,
    At ither's arses!

Thee, Ferintosh! O sadly lost!
Scotland lament frae coast to coast!
Now colic grips, an' barkin hoast
    May kill us a';
For loyal Forbes' chartered boast
    Is ta'en awa?

Thae curst horse-leeches o' th' Excise,
Wha mak the whisky stells their prize!
Haud up thy han', Deil! Ance, twice, thrice!
    There seize the blinkers!
An' bake them up in brunstane pies
    For poor damn'd drinkers.

Fortune! If thou'll but gie me still
Hale breeks, a scone, an' whisky gill,
An' rowth o' rhyme to rave at will,
    Tak a' the rest,
An' deal't about as thy blind skill
    Directs thee best.

ROBERT BURNS, 1785

stells = stills, *blinkers* = spies, *brunstane* = brimstone,
Hale breeks = whole breeches, *rowth* = store.

Burns had a fondness for drink, but his reputation as a drunkard is unjust. His brother Gilbert noted that he never saw Robert drunk until he was 'thrown into society by his fame', and Burns himself mentioned to Dugald Stewart that 'his habitual sobriety was not from virtuous choice'; it was just that too much to drink did not agree with his stomach.

The mention of 'Ferintosh' is interesting. This was the first large-scale distillery recorded in Scotland. We know about it because it was sacked by Jacobite sympathizers in 1689. Its owners, the Forbes of Culloden, were ardent Whigs. When the Whig cause triumphed and 'Dutch' William sat comfortably on the throne of Britain with Queen Mary, Duncan Forbes petitioned the Scottish Parliament for compensation and was granted the right to distil and sell whisky from grain grown on his own lands without paying duty.

Needless to say, he and his successors set about buying up as many adjacent farms as possible, and building more distilleries. By the middle of the eighteenth century, Ferintosh was supplying sixty percent of the legally made whisky in Scotland, earning the Forbes the equivalent of £3 million per annum. The dispensation was withdrawn by Act of Parliament in 1784, the year before Burns wrote 'Scotch Drink'.

> *Gie him strong drink until he wink,*
> *That's sinking in despair;*
> *An' liquor guid to fire his bluid,*
> *That's prest wi' grief an' care:*
> *There let him bowse, and deep carouse,*
> *Wi' bumpers flowing o'er,*
> *Till he forgets his loves or debts*
> *An' minds his griefs no more.*

SOLOMON'S PROVERBS, XXXI 6, 7

THE STRANGE STORY OF WELSH WHISKY
PART I

In September 2001 one of only three surviving bottles from a distillery in North Wales, which closed in 1900, was auctioned. The other two – one of them belonging to the Prince of Wales – are in the Museum of Welsh Life, Cardiff. With the bottle came a collection of framed memorabilia of this vainglorious attempt to produce malt whisky in the Principality.

The photographs have tantalising, and sometimes obscure, captions, such as:

"When Queen Victoria stayed at Pale (near Bala) she was presented with a magnificent polished oak cask, with silver hoops, filled with Welsh Whisky by Mr. Price. A similar presentation was made to the Prince of Wales in 1894. Judging by the letters of enquiry since received from the Yeoman of the Cellars, the Queen is uncommonly anxious to taste her own whisky. Some time after this the whisky styled itself 'Royal' Welsh Whisky."

"The workers at the Frongoch Distillery were brave men to endure the scorn of their contemporaries. Hence the conspicuous and inevitable kettle in the photograph. Since Michael D. Jones, Principal of the Independent College, who started the Patagonian migration scheme[1] lived here at the time, Welsh Nationalism and religious beliefs were so strong that some of the local outside suppliers had to effect delivery by night for fear of being ostracised by their neighbours."

In my subsequent investigations, I am indebted to Dr. Alex Kraaijeveld, who drew my attention to the *Journal of the Merioneth Historical and Record Society*, Vol. IV, 1961-64 (see his interesting contributions to Riannon Walsh's website www.celticmalts.com for more information about distilling in Wales).

The distillery was founded in 1889 at Frongoch, near Bala, in Merionethshire, North Wales, on the bank of the River Tryweryn and adjacent to the Bala-Festiniog railway line. The principal sponsor was the owner of the site and the local squire, Richard John Lloyd Price of Rhiwlas, Esq., "a gentleman who took delight in hunting, in dogs, and in horses", but who also established a slate quarry, a brush factory, a lime kiln, a tile-works and a bottling plant for 'Rhiwalis Table Waters', drawn from St. Beuno's Well, which was promoted under the delightful slogan: "Once drunk, always drunk". The Welsh Whisky Company's founder and first chairman was Robert Willis.

The idea of establishing a distillery in North Wales had come to the two gentlemen two years earlier, while they were strolling in Hyde Park one Sunday. They were especially persuaded by the alliterative attractions of the 'W' – 'Welsh Whisky' flows easily off the tongue, they thought. The company was founded with the considerable capital of £100,000, quickly subscribed by the licensed trade (mainly distillers themselves) in Liverpool, Bristol and London, and was registered on 12th June 1889. Mrs.

Lloyd Price, in traditional Welsh costume, modelled for the company's trade-mark.

All seemed set fair. The situation for the distillery was ideal - "where the fresh ozone breezes tempered the summer heat and moderated the winter cold, where the water supply flowed down from the mountains and the peats were to be found in plenty on adjoining mosses" (*Harper's Manual,* 1915) – and the distillery itself, built from stone collected and carted into Frongoch by local farmers, was described as "one of the most thoroughly perfect that could be for the required purpose" *(ibid).* The same entry refers to the involvement of "the late Mr. Chas.R.Haig – than whom there was no better whisky expert in London and the provinces". (I have been able to discover nothing about this Mr Haig.) Management was entrusted to one Mr Colville, "a Scotchman with a long experience as a distiller"; a Mr Hughes was under-manager – "he had a daughter who was a gifted pianist and her services were much in demand at concerts".

The first season's operations were 'fairly promising'; the second season's even better. Queen Victoria was presented with a cask when she visited Pale Hall, near Bala, in September 1889 (delivered to Windsor Castle two years later), and a similar cask was presented to the Prince of Wales in 1894 by his 'brother freemasons' of Bala Lodge, as mentioned above. He apparently sent a double edged message back through an equerry, to the effect that 'there would always be a place in HRH's cellars for Welsh whisky'. Although Mr Lloyd Price was never awarded the Royal Warrant, the company's advertisements referred to 'Royal Welsh Whisky'.

However, the distillery's success was short-lived. The entry in *Harper's Manual*, 1915 (above) remarks, waspishly, that "The whisky was not maturing properly; it remained rawish, crude and practically flavourless for a pure malt product and a market could not be found for it… In fact, only a year or two sufficed to prove that the very costly experiment of making Scotch malt whisky in Wales, under the best conditions possible, was doomed to failure. The whisky lay at the distillery 'eating its head off' for want of customers, occasional lots of casks were sold off at a loss to get rid of accumulating stock, and ultimately the whole was disposed of at the auctioneer's hammer in London at an average of something less than a half, or even one-third the prime cost of production".

Now, readers of this book will know that the fact that the whisky failed to mature was the fault of the casks, not of the product itself. Although our knowledge of the effects of wood has increased massively during the last twenty years or so, even in the 1890s distillery workers would say "the wood makes the whisky". So what went wrong?

I think the clue is to be found in the picture caption quoted above. North Wales was the power-house of the great Methodist revival of the 1870s, 80s and 90s, and the sect is ardently committed to tee-totalism. This was the era of the so-called 'first religious revival', the high-point of chapel building throughout Wales, although those in the south tended to be Baptist rather than Methodist. The 'Patagonian scheme' was the migration of a ship-load of settlers from North Wales on the S.S. *Mimosa* around 1895, bound for Patagonia (South America) in search of religious freedom and a Utopian agricultural society.

Temperance and Prohibitionist Societies proliferated, indeed the day of the opening of the distillery coincided with a Temperance Meeting in Bala, addressed by Sir Wilfred Lawson M.P., and led to an exchange of doggerel between the latter and the aforementioned Mr Lloyd Price, which included the proud boast:

"And England and Scotia will both cease to boast
When Welsh 'white eye' has got them both simply on toast,
And this still-born idea will not perish still-born,
When Fame sounds Welsh Whisky's praise loud on her horn."

The Welsh Whisky Distillery Co. Ltd was put into liquidation in 1900, and finally wound up in September 1903. The 'most thoroughly perfect' buildings lay empty for some time, then were used as a Prisoner of War Camp 'for many years' during the 1914-18 War. There were still some German prisoners there in late-1919. During the Irish Troubles of the early 1920s it was used to hold Irish prisoners, in the unhappy custody of Scottish guards.

Not a stone remains today of the distillery, and the site was developed for housing in the 1980s.

Afterword

Between 1974 and 1996 a company named variously The Brecon Brewery, The Welsh Whisky Company and Welsh Distillers Ltd operated from Brecon in South Wales. But it did not produce whisky: it bought Scotch fillings and allegedly added herbs to make what it described as 'the original Welsh whisky (or 'chwisgi')'. Following pressure from the Scotch whisky industry, which objected that 'Welsh whisky' was a 'passing off' and a 'misleading indication of origin' under EC Regulations, this company went into liquidation.

In its final incarnation, as Welsh Distillers, it was run by a group of men from Essex, who intended to start distilling – before they too went under, after "cooking the books to delay payment of excise duty" (*Western Mail*, Cardiff, January 2001). The unusual still they commissioned was bought by The Welsh Whisky Company, which has established a distillery in the village of Penderyn in the Brecon Beacons and went into production in August 2000, distilling around 500 litres of malt whisky a day.

PART II

Like all good whisky tales, the story of the revival of distilling in Wales begins in a pub.

It was 1997. Brian Morgan, an economist who was at the time working for the Welsh Development Agency (he is now Director of Cardiff University's Business School), was talking to a friend about the economic future of Wales. Over a couple of malts, they reflected upon the Welsh influence on distilling in the U.S.A., which was considerable – think of famous Welsh names like Jack Daniels and Evan Williams. Would it not be a good idea to approach these companies and see if they would help revive the art of whisky distilling in the Principality?

By chance, two weeks later another of Brian's friends, Alan Evans, phoned to alert him to the sale, in liquidation, of the plant and effects of Welsh Distillers – including a complete bottling line and an unused still.

Welsh Distillers had an exotic history. It evolved out of 'The Welsh Whisky Company', founded in 1974 by the colourful Dafydd Gittins in Brecon. Gittins intended to go into production, and even commissioned a still, but he ran out of money, and the imprisonment of the men from Essex led to the sale of the still and plant. They would go for a song, he said – and they did: £75,000 – and within a year The Welsh Whisky Company Ltd had been incorporated.

The Faraday Still

Their first task was to test and prove the still.

It was of a completely novel design, combining a pot still with elements of a column still, so that complete distillation could be achieved in a single unit (see page 51 for technical description), and was the invention of Dr David Faraday, Professor of Distilling in the University of Surrey, and a great-great-grandson of Michael Faraday, the 'Father' of electricity and magnetism, and the inventor of the electrolytic cell.

The Faraday still also had its origins in a pub – this is the way things work in Celtic countries! – and in a chance meeting between Daffydd Gittins, David Faraday and a colleague of Faraday's from Surrey University, Dr. Ron Schultz. It was the autumn of 1991 and the place was the George Hotel, Brecon. According to Gittins, he told the boffins he wanted "a far more efficient method of distillation for whisky production, [while] Ron and Dave scribbled away on scraps of paper procured from the busy bar maid". In May 1993, the new still was installed as part of visitor centre at the 'Welsh Whisky Distillery', but it was not connected up.

Brian Morgan went to the European Commission for support in testing the novel still. It was of particular interest, since it was capable of producing spirit from any fermented raw materials, anywhere in Europe, with very considerable energy saving over traditional stills (the Faraday still requires only 38% of the energy needed to power equivalent pot stills). The research was led by the University of Surrey, conducted over the course of a year by four Ph.D. students, and funded by the EC and an international consortium of interested companies and academic institutions.

Enter Dr Swan

None of the founding directors of the Welsh Whisky Company had any experience of distilling, so they appointed the leading independent authority on the subject, Dr Jim Swan.

The first innovation that Dr Swan suggested was to do away with mashing and fermenting on site. This is not possible in the manufacture of Scotch whisky, but there is no reason why a pioneering non-Scotch distillery should not have its wash made elsewhere than at the distillery. Conversations were opened with S.A.Brain & Company's Welsh Brewery, in Cardiff, less an hour down the road.

The second innovation came about as a result of the first. Analysing the wash and new-make spirit, Jim Swan felt there was "something lacking". He went back to the brewery to look at their procedures and discovered that, as a matter of course, they sterilize the wash by boiling and thus remove lactic acid (which turns beer cloudy and can introduce unwanted flavours). In whisky distilling, lactic acid (lacto-bacillus) creates a secondary, bacterial, fermentation after the yeast has done its job, and this produces an additional range of flavours and aromas in the distillate.

So when the wash arrives at the distillery (at the moment

20,000 litres is tankered over every eight days) it is pumped into a heated storage tank – lacto-bacillus likes it warm – where lactic acid is added. This would not be allowed in Scotland; Dr Swan maintains it makes for greater control, although similar to what happens in traditional fermentations.

With the help of other experts from the Scotch Whisky Industry – notably Dougie Taylor, Bill Rankin, Paul Ricards and Andrew Kirkby – white oak ex-Bourbon barrels (200 litre) were sourced from Jack Daniels', Evan Williams' and Jim Beam Distilleries, together with a number of ex-Madeira barriques (250 litre) and a handful of ex-Oloroso sherry butts (500 litres) – the latter two as finishing casks.

As governor of Virginia, Thomas Jefferson offered pioneers sixty acres of land in Kentucky if they would raise 'native corn' (maize). Because no family could eat sixty acres worth of corn a year and it was too perishable to transport for sale, much was turned into whiskey, which solved the problem and paved the way for the American whiskey industry. As US president, Jefferson overturned the excise tax that provoked The Whiskey Rebellion of 1794

POINTS OF DIFFERENCE BETWEEN WELSH AND SCOTCH MALT WHISKY DISTILLING

WELSH MALT	SCOTCH MALT
1. Mashing and fermenting done at Cardiff Brewery	Mashing and fermenting done on site (by law)
2. Lactic acid culture added at the distillery to produce a controlledsecondary fermentation	Secondary fermentation follows primary (yeast) fermentation (by law)
3. Single, multi-purpose pot still, with rectifying column	Two pot stills traditional
4. Foreshots run for <1 minute	Foreshots run for 10–45 minutes
5. Average strength of spirit saved (ISR strength): 89%Vol	Average strength 70%Vol
6. Currently produces c.200 litres of spirit a day from 2,500 litres of wash.	Edradour (Scotland's smallest distillery) currently produces c.400 litres of spirit a day from 4,500 litres of wash.

THE PROBLEM OF PROOF

The problem of determining the strength of an alcoholic liquid, or estimating the percentage of alcohol in a liquid, is, according to Sir Walter Gilbey (founder of the wine and spirit merchant W & A Gilbey), 'so complex and so beset with difficulties that its complete solution appears well-nigh hopeless'. But it is a problem of great importance to the taxman, since it provides the basis for duty, 'and the accurate measurement [of alcoholic strength] has always been an obsession of the exciseman'.[1]

Engraving of a pot still, 1873

The Gunpowder Test

As with metals and other materials, the traditional method of measuring the quality of a spirit was by subjecting it to a trial, assay or 'proof'. Several crude methods were adopted. The liquid was vigorously shaken in a bottle and a note was taken of the time it took for the bubbles thus created (known as the 'bead') to disperse. Or the liquor was ignited and the amount which burned away was measured.[2]

The commonest method of 'proving' spirits was by mixing them with gunpowder and setting fire to the mixture. The spirit was deemed to be proved when the mixture ignited; if it did not flash, it was termed 'underproof'. This was a very unreliable test, since if too much liquid was added (even if the liquid was overproof) it would fail to ignite. In truth, it was an arbitrary measurement that really meant nothing more than a standard by which other strengths could be determined.

Nevertheless, proof was the measure for spirit strength until January 1, 1980, when it was replaced throughout the European Union by the simpler measurement of the percentage of alcohol present in a mixture. This measurement was recommended by the Organisation Internationale de Metrologie Legale (OILM: an intergovernmental body established in 1955 to facilitate international trade by harmonization of measurement units) and was based on the European system devised by Joseph Louis Gay-Lussac (1778-1850).

Since then, the strength of spirits throughout most of the world has been measured in percentage of alcohol by volume, or ABV. Thus, the traditional strengths at which whisky was bottled – seventy or seventy-five degrees proof – became forty percent or forty-five percent ABV. At the same time (January 1, 1980), bottle sizes were changed from twenty-six and two-thirds fluid ounces to seventy-five centilitres (cl). In 1992, the standard bottle size was reduced to 70cl.

The United States retains its own proof system, where 100° US proof equals fifty percent ABV at 60°F. Bottles are still 75cl in the US.

The Chemistry of Proof Spirit

Ethyl alcohol weighs less than water, so the chemist can measure the amount of alcohol present in a mixture by comparing its weight to that of the same quantity of water at the same temperature and pressure. This is the 'specific gravity' of the solution.

In 1818, proof was defined by an act of Parliament as 'that which, at a temperature of fifty-one by Fahrenheit's thermometer, weighs exactly twelve-thirteenths of an equal measure of distilled water'.

So the specific gravity of proof spirit at 51°F is .9238 when compared to water; at 60°F, the mixture will contain 49.28 percent alcohol by weight or 57.1 percent alcohol by volume. One hundred percent alcohol, or pure alcohol, is 175° proof spirit (usually termed 75° overproof, although, to further confuse the issue, it was sometimes referred to as a hundred percent proof).

Hydrometers

Given the unreliability of the gunpowder test, and the knowledge that alcohol is less dense than water, scientists devised instruments called hydrometers to measure the amount of alcohol in a solution more accurately.

Archimedes

It is said that the earliest hydrometer was invented by Archimedes (c. 287-212 BC), when he jumped in and out of his bath, realizing that he could test whether gold was pure or impure in the same way. If the displacement of a known weight of pure gold in a tank of water was compared with the same weight of alloy, the latter, being bulkier, would displace more water.

Robert Boyle

It seems that Archimedes' discovery was lost, allowing the English chemist, Robert Boyle to 'reinvent' the hydrometer, which he called a 'New Essay Instrument', in 1675. Like Archimedes' instrument, Boyle's 'common hydrometer' was devised to detect counterfeit coin. It consists of a glass bubble partially filled with mercury or lead shot, with a stem marked with equal graduations. The coin to be tested was attached below the bubble, and immersed in a liquid of known specific gravity (e.g. water); the reading thus obtained was compared with that obtained by a true coin. Boyle's hydrometer was also capable of measuring the specific gravities of liquids, including a solution of alcohol and water, but the instrument was fragile and inaccurate, so was not widely used for this.

John Clarke

The first hydrometer to be designed specifically to determine the density of liquids was invented in 1730 by John Clarke, a Scottish instrument-maker. The bulb was made of copper, with a brass spindle running through it; above the bulb, the spoke was filed flat and marked 'Proof', 'one-tenth over-Proof' and 'one-tenth under-Proof'. Below the bulb, the spindle was cut into a screw, onto which weights of various sizes could be attached, the weight being varied according to the proof of the liquids being examined.

Clarke's hydrometer was adopted by the Excise Board in 1787, equipped with thirty-two main weights and eleven smaller weights (called 'weather weights') to correct variations in temperature. The instrument was not completely accurate, and by adding other constituents (especially sweeteners like molasses) distillers or importers could reduce the reading and thus evade tax. But it was used until the arrival of Sikes' hydrometer.

Bartholomew Sikes

Sikes was secretary of the Excise Board from 1774-83, and at one time collector of excise for Herefordshire. In 1802 (the year before his death), the British government held a competition to find a better hydrometer than Clarke's. A legal decision was only reached on January 17, 1817, and Sikes's widow was paid

£2,000 for the rights.

Sikes's instrument simplified Clarke's by allowing weights to be slid onto the base spindle. It had nine weights, and the upper spindle was graduated into ten equal parts, each subdivided into five. To take a reading, the top measurement was added to the number of the weight, then the reading converted into density and proof by consulting the instrument's accompanying tables.

Sikes's hydrometer was adopted in 1817 by an act of Parliament, and The Spirits (Strength Amendment) Act of 1818 established it permanently. It remained the legal standard measurement until January 1980, when OILM measurements were introduced, but Sikes's hydrometers are still commonly used, notably in spirit safes.

An allusion to the medicinal benefits of whisky, circa 1880

Recent Developments

During the 1980s, electronic instruments were developed for measuring the density of a solution and its alcoholic strength. Called densitometers, these instruments base their measurements on the resonant frequency oscillation of a sample in an oscillation cell. More recently, near-infrared spectroscopy and gas chromatography are also being used in laboratories and larger distilleries. The former is especially useful for measuring the alcoholic strength of whisky-based liqueurs and low-strength 'alcopops': ready-to-drink concoctions.

[1] Philip Morrice, *The Schweppes Guide to Scotch* (Sherborne, 1983)

[2] J Marshall Robb, *Scotch Whisky: A Guide* (Edinburgh, 1950)

PROOF AND ALCOHOL

US proof and British proof compared with alcohol by volume, as measured by the European system.

US PROOF	BRITISH PROOF	% ABV
200° *Absolute alcohol*	175°	100
189.6° *Legal max. whisky strength*	166°	94.8
188° *Av. strength: patent-still spirit*	165°	94
184.8° *Flash-point of spirit (15°C)*	162°	92.4
140° *Av. receiver strength: malt whisky*	122°	70
136° *Av. maturation strength: grain whisky*	119°	68
128°–132° *Av. blending strength*	112°–116°	64–66
126° *Av. maturation strength: malt whisky*	111°	63.4
86° *Av. bottling strength (export)*	75°	43
80° *Legal min. whisky strength;* *usual bottling strength (home market)*	70°	40

The still house at Ben Nevis Distillery, circa 1887

SMUGGLING

"The Scots used to have a reputation overseas for being the one nation in the world who were compulsive smugglers. They acquired it long before the Act of Union…"(Duncan Fraser, *The Smugglers*, 1971)

First, a word about the word. The verb 'schmuggeln' entered the English language from Germany, and in its strictest sense simply means 'to import or export illegally, or to convey secretly', but in Scotland its meaning was immediately extended to describe those who made whisky illegally. 'Illegal' in this context meant 'without taking out a license to distil or paying Excise Duty (in the case of home-produced goods) or paying customs tariffs (in the case of imported goods)'. So a smuggler could be an illicit distiller, the person who transported the contraband around the country or the person who dealt in goods imported from abroad without duty having been paid. In some cases they were all three.

Two branches of government service were set up to police and prevent smuggling: the Commissioners of the Inland Revenue (devoted to collecting duties on excisable goods and to tracking down home-produced contraband) and the Commissioners for Customs (which sought out illegally imported goods). The two departments were only united into Customs & Excise in 1908.

Excise Duty upon spirits was introduced by the Scottish

Parliament in January 1644. After the Restoration of Charles II it was fixed at 1 penny per 'every Gallon of Strong Water or Aqua-Vitae, made and sold, to be paid by the Maker thereof'. This Act also provided for 'Gagers…at all Times, as well by Night as by Day' and empowered them to enter 'the Distilling house' whenever they wanted to 'guage' (i.e. measure) dutiable goods.

Note that to attract duty the spirits must be 'made and sold'. Distilling for home consumption did not attract duty until 1781. There were few dedicated, commercial distilleries in the mid-seventeenth century: distilling was done in the 'distilling house', or 'still-house', just as brewing was done in the brew-house. Large establishments and castles had their own still-houses, often combined with the brew-house; rural communities shared facilities, and sometimes appointed one of their members as distiller and/or brewer. Often this person was a woman.

All this was perfectly legal, but the attractions of making more than was required for community consumption and either selling or bartering it or, commonly, using it to pay the rent were difficult to resist. A shilling's worth of malt could be converted into four shillings worth of spirits. Not only this: the residues from distillation (draff and pot ale – or 'dreg' as it was called) were highly nutritious animal feed; indeed it was reckoned that it was at least as nutritious as grass, so there was an extra incentive to turn pasture into arable land wherever this was possible. Many beasts survived winter only because of winter draff; many landlords provided barley for tenants who lived on barren land, and received their rents as whisky.

To these temptations must be added what might be called 'social pressures'. Working a still was considered a worthier occupation than working the land; distilling illegally was putting one over a Whiggish and unsympathetic government (the Scottish reaction to Mrs Thatcher's poll tax comes to mind); for Jacobite sympathisers, illicit distilling was an article of faith.

In remote parts, especially in the Highlands, whole communities were engaged either in making whisky or in smuggling it to point of sale. It has been estimated that by 1778 300,000 gallons were crossing the Border every year without duty having been paid. The minister of Killearnan, Ross-shire reported in 1796: "Distilling is almost the only method of converting our victual into cash for payment of rents and servants; and what may in fact be called our staple commodity". Two years later, the mighty distiller John Stein gave evidence to a government Committee on Distilling: "There are many who practise this art who are ignorant of every other, and there are distillers who boast that they make the best possible whisky, who cannot read or write and who carry on the manufacture in parts of the country where the use of the plough is unknown and the face of the Exciseman never seen."

Indeed, the officers of the Excise were powerless in the face of such widespread smuggling activity, and when the government increased the number of taxable commodities in order to wage the Napoleonic Wars - including bricks, candles, salt, soap, leather – and repeatedly increased duties on spirits - to such an extent that even legal distillers had to resort to fraud to make ends meet – the situation was close to anarchic. The period between about 1790 and 1823 was the high-water mark of smuggling. The Excise Act of 1823 made it less attractive to distil illegally, while an Act of the previous year substantially increased the penalties for smuggling. Such 'carrot and stick' tactics laid the foundations of the modern whisky industry, and brought to an end an episode in Scottish history which is at once brutal and violent, romantic and heroic.

The United Associate Congregation in St Andrew's, gave a unanimous call on Wednesday last to Mr Ebenezer Halley, preacher of the gospel, to be their minister. The reverend Mr Thom of Anstruther preached, and the reverend Mr Taylor of Ceres presided.

ILLICIT DISTILLATION.—On the evening of the 4th inst. Mr Samuel Milligan, Supervisor of Excise, Paisley, received information that an illicit distillery was at work in a cottage adjoining the Mansion House of Carrdonald. Mr Milligan immediately proceeded to the spot, accompanied by Messrs A. Clerk, E. Cameron, P. M'Lellan, H. Cogan, A. Lang, W. Shorman, and W. Foreman, officers of excise, when they detected a private distillery, carried on with systematic regularity, consisting of one still, contents 60 gallons, one still head, one worm, one worm tub, one mash tun, two wash tuns and 100 gallons of worts, &c. all of which were effectually destroyed. Two of the smugglers were taken before one of his Majesty's Justices of the Peace, for the county of Renfrew, and they having failed to pay the penalty of L30, each were committed to the jail of Paisley. Mr Milligan's exertions in banishing this baneful traffic from our doors, have been indefatigable, for which he deserves the praise of every good member of society.

FIFE CAUSE.—Appeals have been presented to the House of Lords against the decision of the Judges of the Court of Session in Scotland, which lately (confirming the judgment of the Jury Court upon the "issue" directed by the House of Lords to be tried, which was to establish, whether the deeds executed by the late Earl of Fife were his deeds or not) found that these were not his lordship's deeds, and gave the cause

A report of smuggling whisky from
The Scotsman newspaper, *March 1823.*

GOOD HEALTH

*The ancient association between alcohol
(particularly spirits) and health is recollected in many
languages when we drink a person's 'health'.
For example:*

Afrikaans *Gesondheid*

Arabic *Sakh-tain*

Catalan *Salut*

Chinese *Ganbei*

Danish *Skål*

Dutch *Proost*

French *Santé*

Gaelic *Sláinte*

German *Prost*

Italian *Salute* or *cin-cin*

Japanese *Kampai*

Norwegian *Skøl*

Polish *Na Zdrowie*

Portuguese *Saúde*

Russian *Na Zdrovye*

Spanish *Salud*

Welsh *Iechyd dda*

THE RISE AND FALL
OF DISTILLERIES

This section should be read in conjunction with Appendix II on pages 272 to 278.

In 1900, there were 142 operational malt-whisky distilleries and nineteen grain distilleries in Scotland.

In 2004, there are six operational grain-whisky distilleries and ninety-eight malt distilleries, which are either in production (eighty-six), 'mothballed' and capable of returning to production (nine), or planned (three).

Closures generally follow overproduction and broader political, fiscal and economic factors. The table in Appendix II, when read alongside the following summary of what was happening within the Scotch whisky industry and the wider economy, amply demonstrates this.

We may mourn the passing of distilleries – as do the local communities they support – but when all the facts are considered, a degree of inevitability becomes apparent.

1900 – 1920

The 1890s were the greatest boom era for the Scotch whisky industry. To meet demand, thirty-three new distilleries were built during the decade (twenty-one of them on Speyside). Then came a general economic downturn following the end of the Boer War, and investors' confidence in the industry evaporated.

Many distillers sold out to the Distillers Company Limited (DCL), which emerged as the industry leader; it remains so to this day (as Diageo). In order to prevent overproduction, the DCL followed a policy of 'buying up and closing down'. In 1909, Lloyd George's 'People's Budget' exacerbated the problem by raising duty substantially.

With the outbreak of the First World War in 1914, the government effectively took control of distilling, and in 1916, closed all malt distilleries and any grain distilleries that were not producing materials such as acetone for the war effort.

Only one new distillery opened in the period, in 1908: the tiny Malt Mill within the Lagavulin Distillery on Islay, and that was a *jeu d'esprit*.

1920 – 1930

In the aftermath of the Great War, the world went into recession. The British government began to load extra duty on spirits; between 1919 and 1920, duty was increased almost fivefold from seventy-six pence to £3.62 per gallon. Whisky consumption in the UK dropped by one-third.

To make matters worse, the US had ratified the Eighteenth Amendment in 1919, which banned the manufacture and sale of liquor, while Canada, Australia (the biggest export market for

Scotch until 1939), New Zealand and South Africa imposed tariffs and trade restrictions.

Over the course of the decade, three grain distilleries as well as just under forty malt distilleries ceased operation, and three-quarters of the latter never resumed production. Campbeltown was particularly badly hit; of the twenty distilleries which operated here in 1920, only three survived the decade, and one of these, Reichlachan, for only four years.

No new distilleries were built.

1930 – 1960

In the late twenties, the fortunes of the whisky trade began to recover. Prohibition in the States turned out to be a good thing, as demand for Scotch increased massively, and was met by bootleggers, who were well-supplied with good whisky from neighbouring countries like Canada and the Bahamas. By the time repeal came in 1933, the leading whisky companies had their distribution networks in place and were ready to meet the demand.

The depression that had gripped Europe in the early 1930s was passing; sixty-four distilleries went back into production in 1934, and ninety-two by 1939. Five older distilleries closed.

Then came the Second World War. Again, duty was hiked (by £1.25 per gallon immediately, then by a further £3.00 in 1943, which doubled the price of a bottle). In 1940, production was cut by one-third; the following year, grain distilling ceased for the duration of the war, and by October 1943, no grain was available for distilling. The malt distilleries closed as well.

Yet demand for whisky remained high, both at home and abroad, particularly in America. The government allocated a fifth of pre-war amounts of grain to distilling in 1944, allowing thirteen grain and thirty-four malt distilleries to open, with the proviso that the export markets must be kept supplied. At the end of the war, it was decreed that three-quarters of the whisky sold should go abroad.

Stocks of mature whisky had never been lower, and demand never higher; Scotch was now the symbol of the free world. Duty continued to rise. However, in spite of homegrown grain being taken off ration in 1953, and export regulations relaxed the next year, there was an acute shortage of aged whisky. Standard blends were rationed in the home market until 1959, and de luxe blends until the early 1960s.

As the economy recovered from the war, many distilleries that had been silent for decades were re-commissioned; others doubled in size. Two new grain distilleries opened, and the first new malt distilleries since 1900 were built.

1960 – 1980

The boom of the 1960s and early 1970s approached that of the 1890s in scale. Dozens of distilleries were refurbished and expanded; sixteen new malt distilleries were commissioned, as well as two grain distilleries; the output of malt whisky tripled (to 80 million gallons) and that of grain whisky doubled (to 101 million gallons). This was largely taken up by export markets, which tripled in volume between 1960 and 1970.

But then came the oil crisis and the end of the Vietnam War, which had stimulated the American economy. The seemingly inexorable rise in prosperity was abruptly reversed, and recession made a major impact on sales of Scotch, both at home and abroad, leaving the industry massively overstocked.

Towards the end of the 1970s, distilleries began to close once again.

1980 – Present

By 1980, production had far outstripped demand. To compound the problem, the world economy began to slip into serious recession in 1981, and the strength of sterling made export prices uncompetitive. Furthermore, there was a shift in fashion away from Scotch towards white spirits and wine in both the US and the UK, where duty on wine was cut by twenty percent in 1984 while that on spirits was raised by nearly a third. Between 1979 and 1992, wine sales in the UK rose by forty percent, while sales of Scotch declined by twenty-one percent.

Blenders cut their orders for new-make (un-aged) spirit, and distillery closures were inevitable. It began with Ardbeg in 1981 (reopened under new ownership in 1989), which was soon followed by the closure of twenty-one distilleries by the industry leader, the Distillers Company Limited (only six of which have resumed operation). Independent companies followed suit, closing fourteen distilleries, seven of which have re-opened. In 1993, the DCL closed four more distilleries, two of which were eventually sold and have resumed production.

One way of getting round the problem of the decline in orders from blenders was to bottle and sell your malt whiskies as single malts. Until the early 1970s, the few single malts available were not promoted; then brands like Glenfiddich, Glen Grant (in the Italian market), The Macallan and Glenmorangie began to be advertised and made more generally available. This move rapidly found favour with consumers; during the early eighties, the trickle of single malts became a flow, and by 1990, it had become a torrent.

In the last decade, the global market for malt whisky has increased steadily, and the interest and enthusiasm of consumers by leaps and bounds. The whisky industry has responded by releasing long-aged malts, single malts from closed distilleries, and a wide range of 'double-matured' or 'wood-finished' malts (where the whisky has spent the final months of its maturation in a wine cask to give it an extra dimension). The arrival of the first new malt-whisky distilleries for nearly a decade is significant. Two new distilleries have come on stream in the last two years.

Malt-whisky distilling still depends upon the demand for blends; around ninety-five percent of whisky made goes for blending, yet the prospects for both are good.

Glen Grant Distillery, circa 1887

THE AUTHOR'S EARNEST CRY AND PRAYER

TO THE RIGHT HONOURABLE AND HONOURABLE SCOTCH REPRESENTATIVES IN THE HOUSE OF COMMONS

Tell them wha hae the chief direction,
Scotland an' me's in great affliction,
E'er sin' they laid that curst restriction
    On aqua-vitae;
An' rouse them up to strong conviction,
    An' move their pity.

Paint Scotland greetin owre her thrissle;
Her mutchkin stowp as toom's a whissle;
An' damn'd excisemen in a bussle,
    Seizin a stell,
Triumphant crushin' like a mussel,
    Or limpet shell!

Then, on tither hand present her –
A blackguard smuggler right behint her,
An' check-for-chow, a chuffie vintner
    Colleaguing join,
Picking her pouch as bare as winter
    Of a' kind coin.

Is there, that bears the name o' Scot,
But feels his heart's bluid rising hot
To see his puir auld mither's pot
 Thus dung in staves,
An' plunder'd o' her hindmost groat
 By gallows knaves?

ROBERT BURNS, 1786

toom = empty, *chuffie* = fat-faced.

Until 1781, anybody could distil whisky so long as they did not sell it. That year, however, domestic distilling – which most Scots considered to be a human right – was banned by an act of Parliament.

Inevitably, this led to an increase in illicit distilling and smuggling, which was met by further legislation in 1784 and 1786 (the year Burns wrote the poem opposite), enforced by the Board of Excise.

Given the sentiments expressed here and elsewhere in his work, it seems paradoxical that Burns was seeking appointment as an excise officer, even at the very time he wrote his 'Earnest Cry and Prayer'. The truth is that, cheated by his publisher and crushed by debt and a failing farm, government service was one of the very few avenues that offered financial security.

THE 'NOBLE EXPERIMENT'
A visit to America during Prohibition

The prohibition of making, selling, transporting, importing or exporting intoxicating liquors in the United States was enacted by the Eighteenth Amendment to the Constitution, which was ratified in 1919, and came into force in January 1920. The measure was presented to Congress by an obscure Minnesota congressman named Andrew J Volstead, and became known as the 'Volstead Act', although in fact Volstead himself was not a hard-core prohibitionist. Prohibition remained in place until December 1933.

As might be imagined, the Scotch whisky industry was dismayed by the news, especially since, at precisely the same time, the British government raised duty to nearly five times the pre-war level. In fact, Prohibition turned out to be a huge boon. Demand for Scotch increased, and it was perfectly legal for whisky to be exported to countries adjacent to the US, such as Canada and the Bahamas. The whisky companies did not ask what happened to it after that, although they knew very well that it was smuggled into the States in huge quantities. By the time Prohibition was repealed, the foundations of what would become the world's largest market for Scotch had been laid.

The extent to which the Eighteenth Amendment was ignored or circumvented was reported to employees of the Distillers Company Limited in their trade magazine, the *DCL Gazette*

(April 1929) by Francis Redfern, who had recently returned from a three-month tour of the States on behalf of John Walker & Sons. His observations were astute and accurate, and his conclusion was rather like that of the Prince of Wales (later King Edward VIII), who, when visiting New York in 1925 and asked what he thought of Prohibition, replied: 'Great! When does it begin?'

On arrival at his hotel in New York, Redfern noticed '…quite a number of quietly dressed and sad-looking individuals arriving and departing, all carrying suitcases'. 'On inquiry,' he continued, 'I was told that they were bringing in supplies of liquor to the guests. Nobody appeared to take any notice of them… The chambermaid in attendance on my room informed me that practically all the guests in the hotel had liquor in their bedrooms. I found during my stay in the States that this was general.'

Jean Boyer, a French film director en route to Hollywood, had a similar experience. No sooner had he checked into his room than a hand-bill was pushed under his door, reading 'Why come to us? We come to you', and listing drinks from Bacardi (Carta de Oro) at $1.75 a quart to Mumm Champagne at $7.50. When he arrived in Los Angeles, his experience was similar, and here he ordered some good French wine and Cognac. They were delivered in fifteen minutes by a man driving a black Cadillac limousine.

'Whilst staying in Washington, my hotel was invaded by hundreds of men attending a great trade conference,' Redfern reported. 'Most of these men had their private sitting rooms, where they dispensed "Scotch" to friend and foe alike. These congresses are very popular. Some people call them "souses".'

Many of the hotel rooms he stayed in displayed notices which read: 'The proprietors of this hotel have given an undertaking to cooperate with the Authorities charged with the enforcement of the National Prohibition Law' – yet Redfern could still order bottles of Scotch or rye from the 'Captain of the Bell Boys' in these establishments. Another familiar sign was: 'Gentlemen are requested to open their medicine in the bathroom', where there was inevitably a bottle-opener and a corkscrew, both chained to the wall. 'Hotel keepers soon found themselves compelled to defend themselves in this way after the "dry" law was enacted, as guests were known to wreck whole suites of bedroom furniture in desperate efforts to remove a closure,' Redfern observed dryly.

> 'Everywhere I went, people sang the praises of the honest bootlegger. It was clear that no one enjoyed more respect than he, or stood higher in the social hierarchy. I visited many restaurants in New York where whisky is openly served. In private houses where I dined with friends not even remotely connected with our Trade, it was the custom to consume cocktails innumerable before the meal... I travelled hundreds of miles by motor. Every chauffeur I engaged had bootlegged liquor at some time or other and undertook to procure me anything I wanted'.

In some places, the law was not rigorously enforced: 'I consumed beer with my lunch, along with hundreds of other good citizens, including policemen... These things are done openly in some towns.'

But in others, the story was different.

> An American friend with two quarts of Scotch in his motorcar was held up by two Prohibition officers, who pushed automatics into his stomach whilst they secured his 'hooch'. These officers sat up carousing far into the night, whilst my friend languished in his cell. Next morning, in court, the officers were challenged by my friend to produce the bottles. Alas! They could not, since, as my friend wittily remarked, 'They had drunk the evidence'... In one town I visited, they had just sent the principal Prohibition officer to gaol for five years for making "moonshine" in the mountains. In another state I went to, a poor wretch was lying in prison serving a sentence for life for his third offence under the 'dry' law – the offence of "being in possession of one pint of whisky... Each town I visited boasted it was 'the wettest town in the States'.

In cities like New York, drinking was copious, but all 'underground'. As Groucho Marx quipped, 'I was teetotal until Prohibition!' As Redfern explained:

81

'In New York I visited a large number of 'speakeasies' [1] where you could get all the liquor you wanted. There are upwards of ten thousand of these in New York, all paying their "rake-off" to the police and the authorities charged with the enforcement of the law. These speakeasies vary in character from mere drinking dens to palatially appointed private houses, where you find whole families, including children, dining together with utmost decorum, the elders taking wine. Now and again these places are raided by the authorities just to advertise in the newspapers their determination to vindicate the majesty of the law. When the fuss is over, the same place re-opens and everything goes on as before… It rejoices the heart of a bootlegger to be fined. His name and address are then broadcasted [sic] in the newspapers, and he is engulfed in a new wave of prosperity'.

As a matter of fact, Mr Redfern underestimated the number of speak-easies in New York. By the mid-1920s, the city's police commissioner reckoned there were around 32,000 illegal drinking houses – more than twice the number of licensed premises before Prohibition was introduced; a local Congressman put the total closer to 100,000. As Redfern says, some were lavishly appointed and attracted the *beau monde* of flappers, socialites and journalists, like Sherman Billingsley's 'Stork Club', Belle Livingstone's 'Country Club' and 'Texas' Guinan's 'El Fay Club'. Some survived numerous closures to become fashionable, post-Prohibition bars and restaurants; the 'Stork Club' was one, the '21 Club' another. Very many more were squalid dens, selling very poor-quality liquor.

All paid protection money, either to the local gangster boss or to the police. As Charlie Berns, part owner of the successful '21 Club', recollected in an interview:

'Every speakeasy had to make some arrangements with the cops to survive. In our case it wasn't exactly a shakedown – nothing on a regular basis – more like an act of friendship. We would slip the captain a $50 bill from time to time and a box of cigars to the cops on the beat. They could always count on us for free meals and drinks, and at Christmas-time, of course, we had a gift for everybody'.

The old saloons had been male preserves; the speakeasies welcomed women, and the recently enfranchised, 'liberated women' of the 1920s exercised their new freedom wholeheartedly: as much a manifestation of personal liberty as a fondness for alcohol. As one writer observed: '[Before Prohibition] women seldom drank Whisky – at least not in public. But Prohibition changed this… in the speakeasies a generation of college girls learned to drink hard liquor, not because it was available, but because it had become the thing to do.'[2]

Much of the liquor on offer was of poor quality, leading to an explosion in cocktail-mixing. Cocktails were an American invention, and had been around since at least the eighteenth century, but it was Prohibition which was the 'Cocktail Era'. The Eighteenth Amendment gave rise to hundreds of new concoctions, many designed to cover the foul taste of poorly made spirits. 'Everybody with a bottle of bathtub gin, a basket of fruit, and some ice-box leftovers invented a new cocktail. Almost any liquid, short of gasoline, added to the liquor of that era would help conceal its raw alcohol taste and would therefore improve it.'[3]

Redfern concluded his article by saying:

> 'On my last day in New York I walked into the principal book store and said I was prepared to buy all the books dealing with Prohibition they had to sell. They had none. "Prohibition!" said the salesman to me, "Prohibition! Why there ain't no sech thing." Next day I got on board the largest ship in the world, owned by the USA Government. It was bone-dry, not merely until the Statue of Liberty was passed but, after much fuss, scandal and debate in Congress, throughout the voyage... I had no need to worry. You could have filled the swimming bath of that ship with the Champagne and other liquors which were supplied openly to the passengers by the "wine steward" '.

---

[1] The first reference to 'a shop, bar or club where alcohol is sold illegally' as a 'speak-easy' was in 1889, in a New York newspaper, referring to such places in Pennsylvania.

[2] Ed Pearce, *Nothing Better in the Market* [London, 1970]

[3] David A Embury, *The Fine Art of Mixing Drinks* (New York, 1948; London, 1953)

The Whiskey Rebellion reached a climax in 1794 when President George Washington sent in troops to quell those opposed to the excise tax. Yet when Washington completed his second term as president, he tried his own hand at whiskey-making, establishing the George Washington Distillery in 1797. The distillery was one of the largest in colonial America at the time.

HOW TIMES HAVE CHANGED

Today pure malt whisky is rare. To those who can still obtain it, a little water is permissible with the whisky, but preferably after it. Soda water is an abomination and degrades both the spirit and the soul. By and large the connoisseur still abides by the old Highland saying: 'There are two things a Highlander likes naked, and one is malt whisky.'

Personally, I regret the passing of single pot-still malt whisky. I drink it whenever I can find it. But I realize that it is the nectar of the young and the strong, that it goes best with Highland air and with long tramps over hill and moor, and that it is ill-suited to the man who sits all day on an office stool.

SIR ROBERT BRUCE LOCKHART, *SCOTCH* (1951)

Sir Robert Bruce Lockhart (1887–1970) was descended from the McGregors of Balmenach Distillery, and maintained his connections with Speyside all his life. He was a career diplomat, entering the consular service in 1911, and being sent to Moscow, where he became acting consul-general and, in 1918, the head of special mission to the (newly created) Soviet government. In truth, he was working for the British Secret Service, and assisting an attempted assassination of Lenin, and when this was discovered he was sentenced to be shot. He was imprisoned in the Kremlin for six months before being exchanged for Litvinov, who later became foreign minister of the USSR.

During the 1920s and '30s, Lockhart involved himself in banking and journalism, mostly in central Europe, and published five books, including *Memoirs of a British Agent* (1932) – a clue as to what he was really up to – and *My Scottish Youth* (1937). The Second World War found him as British representative to the provisional Czechoslovak government, and later as a deputy under-secretary of state at the Foreign Office (for which services he was knighted in 1943). He retired in 1945. His book *Scotch: The Whisky of Scotland in Fact and Story* (1951) is still in print.

WHISKY AND WATER

There has long been a keen debate about the role that water plays in the manufacture of whisky, the traditional wisdom being that the nature of the water (hard or soft) makes an essential difference to the flavour of the final product.

In the past, production water (usually called 'process water' to distinguish it from 'cooling water': the water which passed through the condensers) was granted semi-magical properties, and even today many distillery owners will proudly mention the source of their water in their promotional materials, as if it made *the* crucial difference to the quality of their brand – far more important than, say, the shape and style of their stills, and how they are operated, or the provenance of the wood in which their spirit matures.

Books about Scotch whisky tend to follow the distillers' lead. To mention three recent publications, Lamont and Tucek consider water to be important enough to warrant a heading in each distillery entry in their *The Malt Whisky File* (1995). Helen Arthur (*Whisky: The Water of Life* [2000]) states categorically 'the water source, whether it is acid or alkaline, hard or soft, plays an important part in the taste and smell of the final single malt'. Consultant geologist Stephen Cribb and his wife Julie open their excellent little book *Whisky on the Rocks* (1998) with the intriguing statement 'Nine hundred billion litres of rain fall on Scotland each year. From this, nine hundred million litres of whisky are made… Of all the ingredients that are combined to produce whisky, the effect of different types of water on the final product is the most mysterious and least-understood factor.'

Even that towering earlier authority, J A Nettleton, in *The Manufacture of Spirits as Conducted at the Various Distilleries of the United Kingdom* (1898) remarks: 'As might be expected, mysterious influences are ascribed by these experienced operatives [i.e. Highland distillers] to the use of moss water [peaty water]'. Elsewhere he makes an intriguing suggestion as to why this might be so:

> Whilst some distillers can safely risk the collection of spirits as low as 10° or 15° underproof [i.e. 48%–51% ABV], many others dare not do so at a lower strength than 40° or 45° overproof [around 80%–83% ABV]. Operative distillers in Scotland usually ascribe this to the action of the moss water used by Highland and Western distilleries for malting and mashing. Their evidence tends to support the view that, where presumably identical materials are used, and where the mashing, fermenting and distilling routine is the same, and nothing differs except the quality of the water used, this great difference of 50° or 60°… is compulsory.

The 'wrong' kind of water can apparently make a huge difference. Another leading authority, Aeneas MacDonald (*Whisky*, 1930) writes:

> There was once a distillery built at considerable expense in a west Highland seaport to make use of the

waters of a burn flowing from a most august moun-
tainside [Ben Nevis Distillery, Fort William]. The water
was all that could be wished for. It was clear and
sparkling to the eye, pleasant to the palate, triumphant
in the laboratory. But alas! It had one fault. Good
whisky could not be made from it. Chemists,
maltsters, and stillmen could try as they might: it was
of no avail… But a mile away was another burn, this
time a mere trickle of water and not particularly
tempting to look at. Despair suggested an experiment
with this water, which came from the same slopes as
the deceiving burn. The result was astonishing – a
whisky of high quality.

Furthermore, the importance of the water source seems to be
amply proved by the fact that so many Highland distilleries were
built on sites formerly favoured by illicit distillers – notwith-
standing the fact that many of these sites were remote. From
Highland Park in Orkney to Lagavulin, Laphroaig and Ardbeg in
Islay; Royal Lochnagar on Deeside to Oban in Argyll;
Glenmorangie and Teaninich in Ross-shire to Aberfeldy and
Tullibardine in Perthshire. And on Speyside: Mortlach, Glenlivet,
Cardow, Balmenach, Aberlour and Tomatin, to name but a few.

Despite all of this, contemporary scientists have grave doubts
about whether the nature of the water makes more than a
trifling contribution to the flavour of mature Scotch whisky. Let
us consider where water impinges upon the production process.
First, it is used in steeping, during the malting process; second,
in mashing (the process water); third, to cool the condensers or

worm tubs (the cooling water, which comes from a different source in some distilleries). Fourth, it is used to reduce the strength of the spirit prior to filling into cask (the reducing water, which is the same as the process water); fifth, in lowering the strength prior to bottling (de-mineralized water is usually used, and the process done at the bottling hall, which is almost invariably on a different site from the distillery). Sixth – should we choose to – water is used in reducing the strength yet again for drinking.

Steeping water is there merely to swell the grains, and is driven off again during kilning. It leaves no residues which might influence flavour, even if the water itself is heavily peated (as at Port Ellen Maltings in Islay).

Process water comes from springs (mainly), lochs, rivers or reservoirs (sometimes private, sometimes providing the public supply). The important factor is purity – the lack of any

An 1887 engraving of Lagavulin Distillery, Islay

contamination; distillers go to some lengths to ensure the purity of their supply, although the water is not treated prior to use (beyond filtering out solid matter). It was always said that soft water was best for making whisky. In truth, this is simply because hard water tends to fur up the pipes and scale the stills with calcium deposits, just as happens in a domestic kettle. Some excellent whiskies are made with hard water, not least Highland Park and Glenmorangie.

Distillation, itself a purification process, removes any character-istics in the water, although it may just be possible that scaly mineral deposits from hard water might make a very small contribution to the flavour of the spirit.

Cooling water does not come into contact with the spirit, but, interestingly, its temperature does make a contribution to the style of the spirit: winter-cold water, especially in worm-tubs, reduces the effect of copper and makes for a heavier spirit. Experienced operators can tell whether their spirit was made during summer or winter.

The purity of reducing water is always checked carefully, but since only a relatively small amount is added to bring the strength down from around seventy percent to sixty-five percent (typically, 63.4 percent ABV – the magic distillers' figure of 111° proof), it contributes nothing to flavour. It has been noted, however, again by Nettleton,[1] although in a different book, that 'The quality of the reducing water affects the appearance and even the flavour of the reduced spirits. A hard water produces a temporary turbidity, especially when added to spirits of high strength.'

He goes on to remark that some distillers, in 1913, softened their reducing water by adding carbonate of soda, which precipitates the lime. Others boiled the water and allowed time for precipitation, or even distilled it prior to using it for reduction.

The water used on the bottling line to reduce to 'bottling strength' (i.e. forty to forty-three percent ABV) is de-mineralized, so adds nothing to flavour.

In the 'water debate', it should be borne in mind that, from mashing to filling takes a matter of days, to be followed by five or ten or twenty years of maturation. This is the time during which the chemistry of the whisky changes dramatically, overwhelming any flavour contributions that might have been made by the water with which the whisky was made.

So the biggest impact that water can make is when you add it to the whisky in your glass. If this water is tainted or chlorinated or over-mineralized, then you will surely taste it; if it is very cold, it will reduce the aroma of the whisky and may affect the taste or 'mouth-feel effect'. Bottled water (the still variety) is safe, and if you use Scottish bottled water, like Highland Spring, it will be soft as well – although I find it somewhat flat compared to good tap water. By 'good' I simply mean tap water that has no aroma or flavour.

A version of this article appeared in the newsletter of the Scotch Malt Whisky Society

[1] J A Nettleton, *The Manufacture of Whisky and Plain Spirit* (Aberdeen, 1913)

WE, whofe Hands are hereunto fet, being the ▮
Britain called *Scotland*, by virtue and in purfuance
Year of the Reign of His Majefty King GEORGI
James Armour Jun. refiding at
to erect, keep, and work, at *Campbelltou*
County of *Argyle* ————— but not
of *Forty* —————————————Gallons E▮
Beer, or Big, of the Growth of the Counties of O
Aberdeen, *Forfar*, *Kincardine*, *Banff*, *Nairn*, and *El*
Clackmannan, and *Perth*, as are to the North and We
runs into the River *Leven*, and proceeding along t▮
of *Stirling*, and from thence, along the great Road
it meets with the great Road from *Kinrofs* to *Perth*
along *the Water of Earn*, till its Junction with the ▮
during the Term of One Year, and for no longer o▮
and to ufe, fell, and difpofe of the Spirits fo diftille
above-mentioned Act of Parliament; he the faid
down the Sum of *ten pounds Sterli*▮
at the Rate of TWENTY SHILLINGS Sterling yearly
and having alfo found fufficient Security for the fu▮
of fuch Penalties as he may incur, in Terms of t▮
GIVEN under our Hands, at the Chief Office of Ex▮
in the Year One thoufand feven hundred and ninet▮

A Dis

A distillery licence of 1791

rt of the Commissioners of Excise in that Part of *Great*
Act of Parliament, made and passed in the Twenty-fifth
hird, do hereby LICENSE, AUTHORIZE, and EMPOWER
Campbelltoun in the County of *Argyle*
in the Parish of *Campbelltoun* . in the
re, a STILL of the cubical Contents, including the Head,
asure, and to distil and draw off Spirits from the Barley,
aithness, Sutherland, *Ross*, *Cromarty*, *Inverness*, *Argyle*, *Bute*,
of such Parts of the Counties of *Dumbarton*, *Stirling*,
ine, beginning at the Boat of *Balloch*, where *Loch Lomond*
Military Road from thence, by *Bucklivie*, to the Town
Tillfoot Road, on the South Side of the *Ochell Hills*, till
long the same, till it comes to *the Bridge of Earn*, and
y, and along that River till it joins the *German* Ocean;
Space, from the Date of this Commission, or Licence;
ct to the Restrictions and Regulations contained in the
mes Armour Jun having paid
being One Quarter of the Composition or Licence Duty,
h *English* Gallon of the Content of the aforesaid Still;
m of FIFTY POUNDS STERLING to answer the Payment
Act of Parliament in that Case lately made and provided.
Edinburgh, this *First* Day of *December*
e *Years* —

icence of 1791.

THE DISCOVERY OF WHISKY

*Down round the southern corner of the dun there was a field of barley all
ripened by the sun. In a small wind it echoed faintly the sound of the ocean; at
night it sighed and rustled as the earth mother thought over things, not without
a little anxiety. It was cut and harvested and
a sheaf offered in thanksgiving, flailed and winnowed, until the ears
of grain remained in a heap of pale gold: the bread of life.*

*In simple ways the grain was prepared and ground and set to ferment; the
fermented liquor was then boiled, and as the steam came off, it was by happy
chance condensed against some cold surface.*

*And lo! this condensation of the steam from the greenish-yellow
fermented gruel is clear as crystal. It is purer than any water from
any well. When cold, it is colder to the fingers than ice.*

*A marvellous transformation. A perfect water. But in the mouth – what is this?
The gums tingle, the throat burns, down into the belly
fire passes, and thence outwards to the finger-tips, to the feet,
and finally to the head.*

NEIL M GUNN, 1935

DON'T BE VAGUE

JOHN HAIG & Co.

GOLD LABEL
LIQUEUR SCOTCH WHISKY

Haig

NO FINER WHISKY GOES INTO ANY BOTTLE

B L

SCOTCH WHISKY

Bulloch, Lade & Co. L
PROPRIETORS.

A CASE OF NO HE

AS
SUPPLIED
HERE

SPECIAL BLEND

GLEN

Royal Liqueur Whisky

★ ★ ★

Ancient Stimulan[t]

Doctor's Orders

"Both-well"

Selected & Bottled by The BOTHWELL BONDING C[o].,

GLASGOW.

ROYAL ARMS
SCOTCH

"HERE'S LUCK TO THE BOSS."

J.G. THOMSON & CO LTD

LEITH, SCOTLAND.

THE FATHER OF ALL SCOTCH WHISKIES

JOHN HAIG & Co. LTD., (owning Haig & Haig. Ltd.) DISTILLERS, MARKINCH, SCOTLAND.

Neil Gunn (1891–1973) was raised in Wick, Caithness, and joined the Excise Service in 1910, working mostly at Glen Mhor Distillery, Inverness. He was friendly with Maurice Walsh (see page 241), who encouraged him to write, and following the publication of *Highland River* (1937), still considered to be a classic, he resigned his job to write full-time. He followed it with another classic, *The Silver Darlings* (1941).

The extract opposite is from an earlier book, *Whisky & Scotland: A Practical and Spiritual Survey* (London, 1935; pages 3–4), in which he also makes the telling comment: 'Indeed, it may be said that until a man has had the luck to chance upon a perfectly matured, well-mannered whisky, he does not really know what whisky is.'

BARLEY VARIETIES

John Barleycorn was a hero bold,
Of noble enterprise;
For if you do but taste his blood,
'Twill make your courage rise.

ROBERT BURNS

I have been told that there are around 300,000 varieties of barley in the world, but that only a few are suitable for making malt whisky. What's more, malting barley is graded on a scale of one to nine by distillers, and only the top three grades are acceptable.

The given wisdom of the whisky industry is that the variety of barley used contributes little or nothing to the flavour of the mature product.[1] It does, however, influence the yield; the amount of alcohol which can be obtained per tonne is based on the barley's capacity to germinate and on its starch content. The variety of barley also influences its 'processability': how well it mashes.

Yield

The earliest kinds of barley grown in the British Isles are termed 'landraces' or 'heritage crops'. In Scotland, it was predominantly a variety called bere: low-yielding but resilient and capable of withstanding the cold, wet climate of the Highlands. Now it is only grown in Orkney and made into bere bannocks, and also a bere beer, or rather, ale.

Bere has four or six rows of seeds in each ear. As early as 1678, agriculturalists recognized that two-rowed barley was better than the coarser four-rowed bere, and in the early nineteenth century, landraces were selectively improved to perform better in specific regions. These were mainly two-row spring barleys; most were weak-strawed and low-yielding, but they did have the useful malting qualities of low dormancy and rapid germination. An example was a variety called Scotch Common.

By the middle of the century, these landraces had been replaced by other selections such as the higher-yielding Chevallier. This, in turn, was superseded at the turn of the century by the dense, narrow-eared Archer and the broad-eared Goldthorpe.

Hybrids

Variety improvement really began at the turn of the twentieth century, with the discovery of hybridization (landrace varieties are by definition improved by traditional methods, not by modern breeding practices). Archer was crossed with Spratt (an old Fenland variety), or Plumage (a Scandinavian variety) to produce Spratt-Archer and Plumage-Archer. By 1940, these were grown in eighty percent of the UK malting barley area.

Improvements in malting barley have been most marked in the last fifty years, when yields have risen by around twenty percent. The leading post-war varieties were Maris Otter and Proctor, but these did not thrive in the harsher climate of Scotland, so the barley was brought up from England (principally Yorkshire and Lincolnshire) and also from Australia, the US, Canada and Denmark. It came by rail, and the same trains took whisky back down south.

Increasing transport costs and the huge demand for Scotch whisky made it imperative to develop a variety which could be grown in Scotland, and the result was Golden Promise: a semi-

This 1909 advertisement for Usher's depicts Demeter, Greek goddess of the harvest, showing the importance of purity in all stages of production, starting with the barley itself

dwarf variety introduced in 1966 which matured early and so could stand the colder, windier conditions of the north. It grew particularly well in the fertile Laich o'Moray, close to Speyside.

Notwithstanding the development of Golden Promise, Maris Otter and Proctor still accounted for slightly over three-quarters of the barley used during the 1970s, and this all came from England. Today, over eighty percent of malting barley is grown in Scotland.

Golden Promise was capable of producing 385 to 395 litres of alcohol per tonne of malt; in 1980, the variety Triumph was approved, producing 295 to 405 litres of alcohol per tonne. This was followed by exotic names such as Camargue (1985), Derkado (1992), Chariot (1992), Optic (1995) and Decanter (2000). Optic accounted for nearly three-quarters of the malting barley grown in 2002, the other leading current variety being Decanter.

Afterthought

It is interesting to note that, in the 1820s, a typical Highland distillery produced around 6,500 litres of pure alcohol per annum, requiring about twenty tonnes of malt, which could be grown on approximately twenty-five acres of arable land. Today, even a medium-sized distillery, such as Lagavulin or Cardhu, produces this amount of alcohol in a day!

---

[1] The leading exception to this view is Macallan Distillery, which makes a virtue of an old-fashioned variety called Golden Promise. Although GP only accounts for a proportion of the malt used by Macallan nowadays, the company maintains that it contributes an 'oiliness', a 'texture', that is an essential part of The Macallan's profile.

MILD AS MILK

Lord Conyngham, the Lord Chamberlain, was looking
everywhere for pure Glenlivet whisky; the King drank
nothing else. It was not to be had out of the Highlands.
My father sent word to me — I was the cellarer — to
empty my pet bin, where there was whisky long in wood,
long in uncorked bottles, mild as milk, and the true
contraband goût in it. Much as I grudged this treasure,
it made our fortunes afterwards, showing on what trifles
great events depend. The whisky, and fifty brace of
ptarmigan all shot by one man, went up to Holyrood
House, and were graciously received and made much of,
and a reminder of this attention at a proper moment by
the gentlemanly Chamberlain ensured to my father the
Indian Judgeship.

ELIZABETH GRANT OF ROTHIEMURCHUS,
MEMOIRS OF A HIGHLAND LADY, 1898

It is a charming thought that George IV drank nothing but illicit moonshine during his visit to Edinburgh in August 1822!

More interesting from a whisky historian's perspective is Miss Grant's mention of maturation improving the quality of the whisky – the first such reference I know of. Her mention of the benefit of being 'long in uncorked bottles' is, however, most mysterious.

The intimate and matter-of-fact style of Elizabeth Grant's (1797–1886) memoirs, begun in the 1850s and not written for publication, has been compared with that of Jane Austen. Her book has remained in print ever since it was first published, a dozen years after her death.

Elizabeth's father was in fact a lawyer in Edinburgh, and he experienced 'considerable professional and financial difficulties until he became a successful judge in India' – thanks to his daughter's good offices.

PEAT

In recent years, the smoky malts from the island of Islay have taken the world by storm. Laphroaig's sales have increased six-fold in seven years; Lagavulin now has to be rationed, such is the demand, and Bowmore won two gold medals and 'Distiller of the Year' at the International Spirits Challenge in September 2002. All three are ranked in the top-ten globally best-selling malts. Ardbeg has tripled its sales in three years, while the last two smoky Islays, Caol Ila and Port Ellen, are less often encountered (although sought after by connoisseurs), the first because almost all its product goes for blending, the second because the distillery closed in 1983.

Not long ago, it was thought that these pungent whiskies were very much an acquired taste. The familiar pattern was to graduate from blended whisky to a gentle malt – a Speyside, perhaps – and only after years of experience to move on to the Islays. An eminent Scottish judge, now deceased, once remarked to a friend of mine that his father would 'never have Islay whisky in the house'; when she raised an eyebrow, he explained that 'it was for outdoor consumption only, powerful and elemental, not for douce [sedate] dining rooms, let alone the drawing room'.

Today, an increasing number of younger drinkers are acquiring a taste for whisky via the big Islays. A recent straw poll I conducted around the bars of Edinburgh showed conclusively that the best-selling malts were Laphroaig and Lagavulin. How do you account for this? Does the contemporary palate, familiar with barbecued spare-ribs and smoked salmon, crave smoky flavours? I think not. I believe it has to do with both the 'obvious' style of these whiskies and their pronounced character.

They are unlike any other drink, including other whiskies, and their character is positive. Whether you like them or not, they are definitely not bland. Their success mirrors that of other 'not bland', full-flavoured products that have become popular in recent years: real coffee and virgin olive oil, farm cheeses and ethnic foods, cigars and cocktails. They are also perceived by younger drinkers as being challenging and aspirational: like jumping out of a helicopter wearing skis or riding a mountain bike over a cliff.

Where does this smoky character come from? It comes from the peat that is burned in the kiln while the malt is being dried. Most distilleries on Islay buy their malt from the maltings at Port Ellen, the island's main harbour, although both Laphroaig and Bowmore have their own small maltings and make around twenty percent of their requirement. Each distillery specifies the degree of peating/smokiness it requires, as we shall see.

Peat is decayed vegetation, decomposed over thousands of years by water, and partially carbonized by chemical change. The word itself is Celtic, reflecting the importance of the material as fuel in these windswept lands. My 1911 edition of *The Encyclopaedia Britannica* informs me that there were then 212,700 square miles of peat bog in Europe. This has been drastically reduced over the last forty years by draining for forestry (particularly in Finland) and (in central Europe) by demand from gardeners.

The vegetation from which peat is made varies slightly from

place to place but usually includes mosses, heather, sedges and rushes; for it to develop, the climate must be cool and wet, the drainage must be poor and the ground ill-aerated. As decomposition proceeds, the vegetable matter becomes waterlogged and sinks to the bottom, piling up and being compressed and carbonized. In some places, the peat layer is as deep as nine metres; some peat bogs are 10,000 years old. Once the bog has formed, the peats are 'won' (to use the correct term) by removing the turf, then digging a trench as deep as the peat layer allows (usually about two metres) and slicing out the peats with a peat spade (a *fal*, in Scots Gaelic; a *slane* in Irish) as from a vast, black pat of butter. The individual peats are then spread out to dry. Peat stacks are still a familiar sight in the west of Ireland and Highland Scotland.

The peats close to the surface are crumbly, rooty and smoky; this is what maltsters want. The deeper peats are darker and burn hotter, and the deepest of all are dry, hard and black – almost like coal. These are the best domestic peats. In Orkney, the various levels are called 'fog', 'yarphie' and 'moss'; in Islay, they refer to 'top', 'second' and 'third' peats, and only use the 'top' peats for kilning.

The smoke produced by peat is highly aromatic and tarry, and if malt is dried over it, these compounds – 'phenols' is the chemical group – coat the grains and imbue the whisky made from them. Laying and tending a peat-fire in a kiln requires considerable skill, and the maltmen at Port Ellen vie with each other to make the most effective fire: one that will pile on the phenols. It must burn slow and cool, since the phenols only attach themselves to the grains during the early stages of kilning, when the malt is still moist; if the fire is too hot, the phenols will themselves be consumed. So there is a limit to the phenolic level achievable, and this is not simply a matter of the length of time the malt is exposed to the peat smoke (although it is clearly an important factor); the big, smoky Islay malts require between four and six tons of peat, burned for between fourteen and twenty hours. In truth, much depends upon the way the wind is blowing and how strongly, and upon the age and nature of the peat.

Degrees of peating are measured in 'parts per million, or ppm, phenols'. The peating specification for Ardbeg, Laphroaig, Lagavulin, Caol Ila and Bowmore is between thirty and fifty ppm. Bruichladdich Distillery at Port Charlotte, which traditionally makes an unpeated malt, is now producing a stablemate, Octomore, peated to sixty ppm (with difficulty). The highest level of peating ever achieved at Port Ellen maltings, experimentally, was just over 100ppm phenols.

The Lowland Scots for smoke is 'reek' – Edinburgh, with its smoking tenements, was once known as 'Auld Reekie' – and after 1824 'peatreek' came to be used to describe illicit homemade hooch, no doubt a reference to the smoky aroma and flavour of such whisky. In the remote Highlands, where peat was the main (in some places, only) source of domestic fuel, the kilning of malt was done entirely over a peat fire. But bearing in mind that phenols will only adhere during the early stages of kilning, before the malt dries out, it is possible to speculate that some homemade whisky was probably not much more smoky than the Islay malts we have been considering.

When defining 'peatreek', *The Oxford English Dictionary* notes: 'The peatreek flavour is really that of amyl alcohol, due to imperfect rectification'. This is nonsense; amyls are part of that other leading group of chemicals found in whisky called 'esters', with characteristics of peardrops, nail-varnish remover and acetone. More commonly (though tasting notes for illicit whisky of the eighteenth and nineteenth centuries are rare) peatreek was described as being 'empyreumatic', which my *Chambers Dictionary* defines as having 'the burned smell and acrid taste that comes when vegetable or animal substances are burned'.

Empyreumatic off-notes can arise in several ways. The most likely cause is driving the still too hard, heating it too fiercely and scorching solid matter in the wash that might stick to its base. After about 1790, large stills were fitted with rummagers – lengths of copper chain-mail, dragged mechanically around the base of the still to prevent solids adhering – but these contraptions were not available to home distillers, and it must have been difficult for them to prevent scorching. Nevertheless, one should not underestimate the skills handed down through generations: Elizabeth Grant of Rothiemurchus, it must be remembered, describes the peatreek she sent up to Edinburgh for the delectation of King George IV in 1822 as being 'mild as milk, and the true contraband *goût* in it' (see page 102). The King drank nothing else, and rewarded Elizabeth's father with an 'Indian Judgeship'.

So perhaps the big Islays, the smokiest of all malt whiskies, recollect the whisky of the past. And perhaps one of the reasons for their current popularity is their 'authenticity', their 'heritage'. An atavistic folk memory, like candles and open fires, Christmas trees and stormy nights.

NOTED FOR ITS GREAT AGE AND PURITY

"HIGHLAND NECTAR"

A BLEND OF THE VERY FINEST SCOTCH WHISKIES.

The Distillers Company Ltd.

EDINBURGH

REGISTERED.

CERTIFICATE OF ANALYSIS.

From Dr CLARK, Public Analyst for the City of Glasgow and the Counties of Lanark and Renfrew, &c.

I have made a minute and careful analysis of a fair Sample of The Distillers Company's "Highland Nectar" Blend of Scotch Whisky, taken by myself from a considerable Stock lying in bond, and the results which I have obtained indicate that it is a pure Whisky which has been well matured in Sherry Wood, and I am of opinion that it is a high-class Whisky of very fine flavour and excellent quality.

CITY ANALYST'S LABORATORY,
GLASGOW, 30TH DECEMBER 1895.

John Clark

An 1895 label for 'Highland Nectar', one of the brands created by the Distillers Company Limited. The brand name reflects the heritage and esteem with which whisky became associated – whether it was 'mild as milk' or the strong, peaty type

THE SELKIRK GRACE

Some hae meat and canna eat
And some wad eat that want it;
But we hae meat and we can eat,
And sae the Lord be thankit.

ROBERT BURNS, 1794

Robert Burns was often asked to pronounce grace before a meal, and expected to extemporize and come up with something new. One might assume that this, his most famous grace, would have been composed in the Border town of Selkirk – but this is not the case.

Burns visited the town only once, on Sunday, May 13, 1787. He was touring with a companion and it was raining hard, so they took shelter in Veitch's Inn, where the local doctor and two friends were sitting by the fire. The innkeeper asked the doctor if the strangers could join them, but he refused, on the grounds that 'they did not look like gentlemen'.

Three days later, Dr Clarkson learned who the stranger was. A contemporary, James Hogg ('The Ettrick Shepherd') wrote that 'his refusal [to allow them to join him] hangs about the doctor's heart like a dead weight to this day, and will do till the day of his death, for the bard had no more enthusiastic an admirer'. Such are the rewards of snobbery!

The grace itself was probably first delivered at the Heid Inn in Kirkcudbright High Street, in the presence of Dunbar Douglas, 4th Earl of Selkirk, in July 1794 (the inn is now named the Selkirk Arms). It is also possible that the grace was traditional, and not in fact composed by Burns at all. He certainly never wrote it down. And while Burns himself never drank much whisky, the Selkirk Grace has come to be traditionally said with Scotch.

MALTINGS

Barleycorns are mainly starch. To make alcohol, this must be turned into sugar and fermented with yeast. Malting does not effect the conversion into sugar, but it prepares the starch for conversion by breaking down the tough cell walls and proteins which bind the starch cells, and by activating enzymes in the grains which will do the job of conversion when hot water is added to the ground malt in the mash tun. I have heard it compared to unwrapping a sweetie prior to eating it.

In nature, the cell walls break down when the plant begins to grow. The maltster tricks the barleycorns into believing that spring is here and it is time to germinate. He does this by steeping the grains in water, resting them (moist) so they begin to sprout and then stopping the germination by drying them (now called 'green malt') after the cell walls have gone, but before the new plant has consumed any of the starch.

Floor Maltings

Until the twentieth century, this process was carried out in so-called 'floor maltings', and every distillery made its own malt. In floor maltings, the damp grain is spread out on a cool (cement or slate) floor to the depth of between one and two feet. Germination generates heat, so the grain has to be regularly turned with wooden shovels and rakes to keep the temperature even, and to prevent the little rootlets becoming entangled and matting. This was a laborious task, and tended to develop a repetitive strain injury called 'monkey shoulder' among maltmen. After about nine days (depending on the ambient temperature; it will be less in warm weather, more when it is cold) the cell walls will have broken down and the green malt is ready for kilning.

In the Lowlands, malt kilns were fuelled by anthracite and coke; in the Highlands and Islands, where peat was the universal fuel, this fired the kilns and the fragrant peat smoke made an important contribution to the flavour of the whisky (see 'Peat', pages 102–111).

Drum Maltings

As early as 1885, engineers turned their attention to inventing a method of mechanical malting which would do away with the manual handling of the grain and better control temperatures, so as to produce more even germination, and thus better malt.

The key to such methods was aeration, and the systems are generally referred to as 'pneumatic'. A pneumatic system employing cast-iron cylinders or 'drums' was invented by a Monsieur Galland, and perfected in London during the 1890s by the Scottish engineer R Blair Robertson. Early drums held only from 2.5 to 10.5 tons of grain (today, they typically hold 100 to 300 tons). They were mounted longitudinally, and within each was another, perforated drum which was capable of being rotated. This was half-filled with barley.

In the first stage, the grain was cleaned and steeped by being revolved through a shallow trough of water, while being simultaneously aerated. Next, the water was drained off and the grain 'rested' and encouraged to germinate: aerated by a fan at one end of the drum, sprayed occasionally with fresh water and turned automatically from time to time to ensure even 'modification'. Once conversion was complete, the green malt – 'sweet and fresh, without mould or any damaged corns'[1] – was transferred to the kiln for drying. Later, the drums were adapted to dry the malt as well. Called SGKVs (Steeping, Germination and Kilning Vessels), these are now the most common method of malting

A Galland pneumatic drum was installed at Glen Grant Distillery in the 1890s and at Speyburn in 1905. The latter was described as a 'very compact unit with a central belt-drive mechanism to turn the drums and the ventilation fans, with a double-deck kiln for fuel efficiency'. It was successfully operated for sixty years by the Distillers Company. Drums were also introduced at St Magdalene Distillery, Linlithgow, in the 1920s and operated successfully until the 1950s. But it was in the manufacture of grain whisky that they were mainly used; even by 1913, J A Nettleton was able to remark that 'such methods were in general use at distillery maltings, especially at patent-still distilleries'. Most malt distillers stuck with floor maltings, however.

Saladin Maltings

Around the same time as drum malting was being perfected (i.e. the 1890s), another form of mechanical malting was invented by Charles Saladin, called the 'Saladin box'. This was simply a concrete trough equipped with revolving rakes; in it, the barley was steeped, turned by the rakes and mechanically aerated. The method was quickly taken up by the brewing industry in Europe, but, as with so much else, the whisky industry held back for fifty years.

The first distillery to install Saladin boxes was North British, in 1948 – not without teething problems (the works manager was sent to Copenhagen to 'ascertain the best methods of overcoming the difficulties of condensation'). Further boxes were installed at North British in 1963. Glen Mhor Distillery, Inverness, followed in 1949, and Tamdhu in 1950 (where they are still in use). Dalmore Distillery, Alness, installed them in 1956, where the mechanical turners were of a different design, and Glen Moray, at Elgin, in 1957. Around ten malt distilleries installed Saladin boxes in the 1950s and early 1960s, including Dailuaine (1959–60), Glen Albyn (1961), Ord (1961) and Imperial (1967).

Centralized Malting

But even by the early sixties, on-site distillery maltings were doomed, whether floor, Saladin or drum. The phenomenal growth in demand for Scotch after the Second World War created such a demand for malt that they could not cope, and in a short period most distillery maltings closed, malt being bought in from dedicated, centralized maltings.

In 1968, Scottish Malt Distillers (or SMD, the malt-whisky production division of the Distillers Company Limited) ceased floor malting at twenty-nine distilleries. Two years before, the company had built a huge drum malting at Burghead, on the Moray Firth, and the same year the maltings at Muir of Ord were substantially expanded, with six drums added to the existing Saladin boxes. (Ord Distillery itself used malt from the boxes; the drums met the requirement of SMD's seven distilleries in the north of Scotland.)

SMD followed this by building a seven-drum malting adjacent to its Port Ellen Distillery, Islay, in 1973, and at Roseisle in 1979–80. Both these plants have the ability to produce peated malt – a capacity which most of the new maltings did (and do) not have. Roseisle was the first fully automated malting to be used in the UK.

Other distillers also centralized their maltings. For example, Hiram Walker's subsidiary, Robert Kilgour, built a large drum malting at Kirkaldy in 1968, and the same year Inver House Distillers opened 'the largest commercial malting plant in Europe' at its Moffat distillery, Airdrie. Independent maltsters like ABM, Bairds, Moray Firth, Simpsons and Pauls followed suit to supply the independent whisky companies.

Afterthought

There is no doubt that centralized, pneumatic maltings produce a more reliable product than the old floor maltings, although those distilleries that retain their floor maltings believe they allow for greater control of the level of peating. Some years ago, Highland Park closed its maltings for a season and bought in all its malt requirement, peated to the specified level with Orkadian peat, but it did not produce the character of spirit desired and the company resumed in-house malting.

Let Neil Gunn have the last word:

'In all this malting process, skilled judgement is needed, for the goodness of the malt determines not only the quantity of alcohol that may result from its fermentation but the quality of the ultimate distillate itself'.

---

[1] Sleeman, quoted by J A Nettleton (*The Manufacture of Whisky and Plain Spirit* (1913)

MALTINGS CURRENTLY OPERATING IN SCOTLAND

Bairds   Arbroath, Angus; Moray Firth, Inverness; Pencaitland, East Lothian

Bass   Alloa, Kincardineshire

Crisp   Portgordon, Banffshire

Diageo   Burghead, Morayshire; Glen Ord, Inverness-shire; Port Ellen, Islay; Roseisle, Morayshire

Kilgour   Dunnikier, Fife

Pauls   Buckie, Banffshire; Carnoustie, Angus; Glenesk, Angus

Scotmalt   Kirkliston, West Lothian

Simpsons   Berwick on Tweed

DISILLERIES WITH MALTINGS

Balvenie   floor malting; supplies 10% of requirement

Bowmore   floor malting; supplies 20% of requirement

Glen Ord   Saladin and drum maltings; supplies 100%
                        of requirement and the requirements of six
                        other distilleries

Highland Park   floor malting; supplies 20% of requirement

Kilchoman   floor malting; supplies 100% of requirement

Laphroaig   floor malting; supplies 20% of requirement

Springbank   floor malting; supplies 100% of requirement,
                        and the requirement of Longrow and
                        Glengyle

Tamdhu   Saladin malting; supplies 100% requirement,
                        and most of the requirement of Glen Rothes

Glendronach   still has its floor maltings, but they have not
                        been used since 1998

MORE THAN JUST A DRAM

Take clear water from the hill
and barley from the Lowlands,
take a master craftsman's skill
and something harder to define,
like secrets in the shape of coppered still
or the slow, silent, magic work of time.

Chorus

Whisky, you're the Devil in disguise,
at least to some that's the way it seems,
but you're more like an angel in my eyes,
catch the heady vapours as they rise
and turn them into dreams.

Bring home sherry casks from Spain,
Sanlúcar de Barrameda,
and fill them up again
with the spirit of the land.
Then let the wood work to the spirit's gain
in a process no one fully understands.

Repeat Chorus

Now, the spirit starts out clear
but see the transformation
after many patient year
when at last the tale unfolds,
for the colours of the seasons will appear,
from palest yellow to the deepest gold.

Repeat Chorus

When you hold it in your hand
it's the pulse of one small nation;
so much more than just a dram,
you can see it if you will –
the people and the weather and the land,
the past into the present is distilled.

Whisky, you're the Devil in disguise,
at least to some that's the way it seems,
but you're more like an angel in my eyes,
catch the heady vapours as they rise,
and turn them into peaceful, pleasant dreams.

ROBIN LAING (1995)

Robin Laing is one of Scotland's leading singer-songwriters. He has also recorded two CDs of whisky-related songs and poems, *The Angel's Share* (1997) and *The Water of Life* (2003), and has published a seminal collection of poems and songs about whisky, *The Whisky Muse* (2002). The author tells me that *More Than Just a Dram* was begun on the island of Eigg and finished on the island of Islay.

THE FIRING OF STILLS

Stills may be heated in two ways: directly (with a naked flame beneath) or indirectly (by steam-heated pans and coils within the body of the still itself, not unlike an electric kettle). A form of indirect heating by steam is employed by patent stills, and as early at 1888-89, the Glenmorangie Distillery installed steam coils: the first malt distillery to do so, and possibly the only one for many years,[1] for indirect firing was not generally adopted by the whisky industry until the early 1960s. Indeed, direct firing was considered to be one of the key factors in distinguishing malt whisky from patent-still grain whisky, and one malt from another. Thus, Sir Walter Gilbey was able to write in 1904:

> 'It is a curious fact that the heat of the fire [in pot-still distillation] also imparts a Flavour to the vapourized matter. The fire heat gives the spirit a character which distinguishes it from Spirits distilled by the Patent Still. It imparts to the Spirit the character known as empyreumatic, which is easily recognized in the product of the Pot Still and which is quite absent in Spirit produced by the Patent Still'.

Nearly half a century later, in 1951, the inaugural lecture of the Wine and Spirit Association of Great Britain expanded upon this view:

'The Still is heated by a naked fire, and it follows inevitably that the heat applied is not constant at all times or at all portions of the Still in contact with the fire. It is this unequal heating in parts which is believed to cause changes in the Whiskies which distinguish one from the other, and it is generally considered that the process of slow heating of the Still bottom and of the wash contained in the Still is a vital factor in developing the character and quality of Scotch Whisky, and bringing out its special peculiarities… Brandy is also distilled over a naked fire, and I understand that many brewers prefer a naked fire to other, and perhaps more scientific, methods of heating, so probably there is something in the use of a naked fire which has a good effect, even though we don't know why'.

Distillers who have worked with both direct and indirect-fired stills are agreed that the spirit produced by the former was heavier. Ian Henderson, for example, whose first job in the whisky industry was at Strathisla Distillery, recalled that there were two pairs of stills, one pair coal-fired and the other steam-fired. 'The two spirits were completely different,' he explained. 'Direct-firing produced much more body in the spirit.' It was the company's policy to vat the two makes together to create Strathisla single malt.

The Rise of Indirect Firings

Direct-fired stills were dirty, difficult to run and extremely labour-intensive, however. The fire had to be controlled physically by raking out the furnace or damping down with a hose when the boiling point was reached. Soap was often used in the wash stills as a surfactant, but in spite of this, it was not uncommon for the wash or low wines to rise up into the neck of the still and carry over into the 'worm' or condenser.

In the late 1950s and early 1960s, many distilleries installed mechanical stoking systems, and some even experimented with oil-firing (notably Ord and Tomatin Distilleries), but this was later abandoned, since it caused the base of the stills to become brittle. Gas-firing, by North Sea gas, both natural and petroleum by-product, proved more successful and remains in use at Macallan Distillery.

As part of the general refurbishment and expansion that took place during the boom years of the 1960s, all but a handful of malt distilleries went over to indirect firing. In wash stills, the usual method of heating is via thin-walled cylinders, called 'kettles', while in spirit stills, coils are more generally used. Some, like Glenfarclas Distillery (which remains direct-fired to this day), experimented, then retained the traditional method. In Glenfarclas's case, one spirit still was converted to steam coils for a week in 1980, but, in the words of John Grant, the distillery's owner, 'The spirit it produced was not Glenfarclas – it had no guts.'

Conversion is not done lightly. Certainly in more recently

converted distilleries, months of tests are done to adjust the production regime and cut points so as to make sure the liquor made from indirect-fired stills has the same characteristics as that from the old, direct-fired plant. Nevertheless: 'There is general agreement that steam heating and the installation of tubular condensers both tend to result in the production of a more lightly flavoured spirit.' [2]

Engraving of a whisky still from 1729

---

[1] An early twentieth-century steam-jacketed still survived at Auchentoshan until 1975

[2] Professor R K Martin, Dr E B Duncan and John R Hume, *The Development of Scotch Whisky Plant and Associated Processes* (in *The Scotch Whisky Industry Record*, Dumbarton, 1994), p. 370

REMAINING DIRECT-FIRED STILLS IN THE UK

Glenfiddich
Gas-fired (coal-fired until 2002–03);
ten wash stills, eighteen spirit stills

Macallan
Gas-fired

Glendronach
Coal-fired; two wash stills, two spirit stills

Glenfarclas
Gas-fired since 1972; three wash and three
spirit stills

Springbank
Oil-fired, wash still (which also has steam coils);
two low-wines stills indirect-fired)

Glen Grant and *Longmorn Distilleries* were
converted to indirect firing in the late 1990s,
Ardmore in 2002.

MEMORIAL

CONCERNING THE

𝔐𝔞𝔩𝔱=𝔗𝔞𝔵.

EDINBURGH,
Printed in the Year M. DCC. XXVI.

[Price Three Pence.]

A pamphlet from 1726, 'mourning' the demise of the malt tax which had been proposed by Chancellor of the Exchequer Robert Walpole

LIVING FOREVER

If a body could just find oot the exac' proper proportion and quantity that ought to be drunk every day, and keep to that, I verily trow that he might leev for ever, without dyin' at a', and that doctors and kirkyairds would go oot o' fashion.

THE ETTRICK SHEPHERD
– QUOTED BY CHRISTOPHER NORTH (1826)

'Christopher North' was the pseudonym of John Wilson (1785-1854), who was editor of *Blackwood's Magazine* and, after 1820, professor of moral philosophy in the University of Edinburgh. 'The Ettrick Shepherd' was the poet James Hogg, author of *The Confessions of a Justified Sinner*.

Under Wilson's editorship, *Blackwood's* became famous for its fearless polemics, savage reviews, literary jokes and wide-ranging conversations. The latter – from which the above quotation is taken – were set in Ambrose's Tavern (which stood on the site of what is now Edinburgh's Café Royal), and were reported in the long-running column, *Noctes Ambrosianae*.

James Hogg (1770-1835) was born in the Ettrick Valley and spent his youth working as a cowherd and shepherd, before educating himself and publishing a number of celebrated poems. He came to Edinburgh about 1818 and published a series of notable supernatural novels (all still in print), including the famous *Confessions of a Justified Sinner* (1824).

WORMS

In the early days of distilling, alcohol vapour was condensed simply by the surrounding air: the solution of water and alcohol was heated in an alembic, the alcohol vapour (since it boils off first, at 78.3°C) came over the neck of the still and passed down a beak-like tube called a cucurbit (today we would call it a 'lyne arm' or 'lye pipe'), where it condensed back into liquid. Sometimes there was a water bath around the head of the still, but it was only in the mid-1500s (1540–50) that the lower end of the lye pipe was placed in a tub of water: first straight across, then diagonally and finally in a coil, which increased the cooling surface available and allowed the distiller to produce more spirit.

This is the 'worm'. The earliest written reference to it in English is in *The Art of Distillation* by John French (1651): 'Put it into a Copper Still with a worme'. Yet around a hundred years earlier, Adam Lonicer's *Naturalis Historiae Opus Novum*, published in Frankfurt, included an illustration of a worm and worm-tub.

Until the late nineteenth century, worms were the only form of condenser available to distillers: a coiled pipe in a tub of cold water. In whisky distillation, the pipe was (and is) made of copper, not only because copper is more malleable, but, more importantly, because the chemical reaction which takes place between the distillate and the copper purifies the former and lightens the spirit.

In the 1880s, variations on the traditional worm-tub were

invented, forerunners of the 'shell-and-tube' condenser that would later become the most common condensing method. The shell-and-tube condenser is a bundle of narrow-bore copper pipes, arranged in parallel within a copper canister. Alcohol vapour fills the canister and condenses on the copper pipes, through which cold water is passed. This requires less water than worm tubs, the plant is easier to clean and replace, and as condensers permit greater contact with the copper, the spirit produced is purer and lighter in character than that produced by worms.

Yet the whisky industry was slow to adopt this new method. Alfred Barnard, later editor of the trade journal *Harper's Weekly Gazette,* who toured all the distilleries in Britain and Ireland during the mid-1880s,[1] mentions only eight that were equipped with condensers. Glenugie, Bowmore, Milton (i.e. Strathisla) and Strathdee used their condensers in parallel with traditional worm-tubs; the wash still at Glenugie Distillery, Peterhead (built in 1875), had 'a Horizontal Condenser of a very modern design, having 200 tubes in it, the one for the Spirit Still being of the ordinary upright kind, with 50 tubes', while Bowmore had two condensers and three worm-tubs. At Kirkliston Distillery, near Edinburgh (est. 1795), 'six sets of Willison's Upright Condensers, and a Worm Tub of a most primitive pattern' provided for six pot stills. Condensers were also noted in passing at Dean, Edinburgh (built 1881), and Ardbeg, Islay (est. 1815). Barnard's book also contains advertisements from two companies listing condensers among the other distilling and brewing equipment they manufactured. During the boom of the 1890s, when forty new distilleries were built, one might have thought that shell-and-tube condensers would have been the norm. This was not the case. In 1913, J A Nettleton could still remark:[2]

'It is abundantly evident that the old-fashioned worms and worm-tubs are doomed to disappear, and that far more convenient apparatus will take their place. Upright condensing cylinders or boxes, 6 to 10 feet in height and 1.5 to 2 feet in diameter, afford, in many cases, sufficient condensing and cooling power for the various vapours and liquids from a large still'.

It was not until after World War II that shell-and-tube condensers became common, and even then they were not adopted wholesale. The pioneering distillery architect Delmé Evans incorporated them into his designs for Tullibardine (1949), and later Macduff (1960), Jura (1960–63) and Glenallachie (1968), as did Sir Albert Richardson in his designs for Tormore (1958–60), but worm-tubs were installed at the strikingly modern Glen Keith Distillery (1957–60).

However, when building regulations were relaxed in 1960, many whisky companies embarked on large-scale refurbishment and expansion to meet the rapidly growing demand for Scotch. Engineers and accountants at Scottish Malt Distillers, the production division of the mighty Distillers Company Limited, embraced shell-and-tube condensers enthusiastically and installed them whenever they were expanding or replacing plants in their forty-five distilleries. The independent malt-whisky producers pursued a similar policy during the same period and expanded their distilleries, some to double their capacity, and all with condensers.

By the late 1970s, only a dozen or so distilleries had their original worm-tubs, although in at least one case – at Dalwhinnie, in 1996 – worm-tubs were reinstated, at considerable expense. The relevance of this to the consumer is that the spirit produced by worm-tubs is heavier than that produced by condensers, for the simple reason that the spirit vapour has greater contact with copper (a purifier) in condensers than in worms. During the winter months, when the water in the tub is colder, there is even less copper uptake in the worm, so the spirit is even heavier.

In the days of 'dramming', when distillery workers were issued with approximately a gill of new-make spirit at the end of their shifts (two or even three times a day, with extra rations on the completion of 'dirty' jobs), they could tell whether the spirit had been made during summer or winter. Dramming was stopped by health and safety regulations during the 1970s.

So whisky made by distilleries with worm-tubs is likely to be heavier in texture, and some would say, more characterful, although much depends upon other features (such as purification devices) and the distilling regime. If the stills are run hot and fast, there will be greater copper contact.

[1] Alfred Barnard, *The Whisky Distilleries of the United Kingdom* (London, 1887)
[2] J A Nettleton, *The Manufacture of Whisky and Plain Spirit* (Aberdeen, 1913) p.493

DISTILLERIES THAT STILL USE WORM-TUBS

Balmenach

Benrinnes

Cragganmore

Mortlach

Dallas Dhu
*Now preserved as a museum
by Scottish Heritage*

Dalwhinnie
*Worm-tubs removed
1985; reinstated 1996*

Edradour
*Still operates a worm
installed in 1825*

Glen Elgin

Glenkinchie

Oban

Rosebank
Wash-still only; closed 1993

Royal Lochnagar

Speyburn

Springbank
Wash-still only

Talisker

Above from left: George Ballantine (1809-91),
Johnnie Walker (1805-57), Andrew Usher II (1826-98)
and John Dewar (1806-80).

Glendarroch Distillery, Ardrishaig, 1887

RECTIFICATION

To 'rectify' is to 'put, set or make right' – from the simple Latin rectus, 'right' and facere, 'to make' – but in distilling parlance and the language of chemistry it means 'to purify by (further) distillation'. The 'further' is implied: first one distils, then one rectifies to purify, refine and strengthen the spirit by repeated distillation.

The earliest reference to 'rectification' in Scotland that I know of is in Martin Martin's *Description of the Western Isles* (1703) where he describes the natives of Lewis as brewing 'several sorts of Liquors, as common *Usquebaugh*, another call'd *Trestarig, id est, Aqua-vitae*, three times distill'd, which is strong and hot; a third sort is four times distill'd, and this by the Natives is call'd *Usquebaugh-baul, id est Usquebaugh*, which at first taste affects all the Members of the Body: two spoonfulls of this Last Liquor is a sufficient Dose; and if any Man exceed this, it would presently stop his Breath, and endanger his Life.'

From the 1770s, the majority of Scottish grain spirit (made in pot stills before the 1830s), was sent to England for rectification and 'compounding' into gin. This had begun in 1777, when 2,000 gallons were sent south; by 1786 the amount was 882,000 gallons – nearly a quarter of the English spirits production.

'Compounding' means the addition of sugar, herbs, spices, fruits and other 'botanicals'; in truth, much of the spirit sent south was crudely distilled and required rectification to make it potable. The gins of the day were heavy and cordial-like, sweetened with sugar and glycerine and strongly flavoured with juniper in order to disguise the rough and empyreumatic flavour of the base spirit. Even in Scotland much spirit was compounded with fruits and aromatics – so much that 'usquebaugh' was defined by Dr. Johnson in 1755 as 'a compounded distilled spirit, being drawn on aromaticks; and the Irish sort is particularly distinguished for its mild flavour. The Highland sort is somewhat hotter, and by corruption in Scottish they call it *whisky*'. *

After the invention of the patent or continuous still around 1830, the spirit was technically already 'rectified' to a very high strength and purity – to this day the second column of a continuous still is called the 'rectifier' – but it was still rectified, or re-rectified, and compounded to make good gin and other liqueurs. Cheaper gins merely added essences and flavouring to the spirit, as happens today, but the better gin houses took advantage of the improved spirit to invent the 'London Dry Gin' style: unsweetened, clear, less aromatic. Gordon's, Booth's, Burnett, Tanqueray and Burroughs were all in existence by the 1860s.

'Rectification' also embraces 'one who rectifies'. Samuel

---

* This early definition in Johnson's *Dictionary* – whisky = a compounded spirit – has led to all kinds of confusion. In truth, it would seem that the good doctor got it wrong. By the 1750s other writers were distinguishing usquebaugh, a compounded spirit, from 'plain malt spirits, commonly called Aqua Vitae' [the Seafield Papers, 1751]. The writer of the latter goes on: 'nor have these plain malt spirits such bad effects on the health of those who drink them as compound spirits in England there being few or no instances of any suffering by the use of them'.

Morewood (*The Inventions and Customs in the Use of Inebriating Liquors, 1824*) maintained that because of the coarseness of English spirits owing to the 'grossness and richness of the wash', 'a number of traders, denominated rectifiers, were called into action between the distillers and the consumers. These rectifiers re-distilled the spirits with the addition of certain drugs and flavouring materials, such as juniper berries, spirits of turpentine, etc., by which they made a sort of compound called British Gin; or else with spirits of nitre, prunes, etc., manufactured an imitation of Brandy and Foreign Liqueurs.'

All Scotch spirits sent to England went through the rectifiers, 'who held the position of arbiters of public taste'. Their monopoly was only broken by the Chancellor of the Exchequer in 1823, the liberal Earl of Ripon, who saw that if distillers were encouraged to make 'good pure spirit', the liquor would 'unquestionably be more palatable and wholesome in the natural state, than when compounded and impregnated with such materials'. An interesting and important side effect of the seminal Excise Act of 1823, which laid the foundations of the modern whisky industry.

VATTING

A vat is simply a large vessel for holding liquids. It shares the same root as 'fat', the Old English word 'faett', rendered as 'fat' in Old Norse, 'vat' in Dutch and 'fass' in German. Maybe it carries the implication that a 'vat' is a 'fat' tun – the last was current one hundred years before the Norman invasion.

The verb 'to vat' simply means 'to put into a vat', but in relation to whisky it has gathered other meanings or implications, and these have changed slightly over the years, which makes the word worthy of our consideration.

Until a hundred years ago, at least, 'vatting' was synonymous with 'blending', and this was generally called 'mixing'. 'Vatted whiskies were 'mixed' whiskies were 'blends'.

The first-ever brand of Scotch whisky is generally recognised as being *Usher's Old Vatted Glenlivet*, introduced in 1853. Until 1860, and possibly for longer, this was a 'vatting' of malt whiskies only, then it became a mix of malts and grains, without a change of name. Around the same time, Charles Mackinlay introduced Old Vatted Ben Vorlich, but we don't know whether this was pure malt or a blend of malts and grains.

We have the authority of the distiller and author, Charles Tovey (*British & Foreign Spirits*, 1864) for the use of the term blend: "The prevalent notion among whisky drinkers, especially in Scotland, is that several varieties of whisky blended is superior to that of any one kind." He does not specify whether the blend is of malts only or of malts and grains.

When William Sanderson invited a group of friends to his offices in Leith in 1882 to sample a number of 'vattings', he was clearly referring to blends of malt and grain whisky. His friends chose the sample from 'Vat 69', and the rest is history.

But by 1900 there is evidence that the term 'vatting' was being differentiated from 'blending' ('mixing' had long-since disappeared from the blenders' vocabulary), J L Anderson, the author of the (unpublished, so far as I am aware) *History of the House of Dewar*, reports in 1901: "Hitherto our blending had been done on the primary principle of mixing all single Whiskies at once and completing the proprietary blend in one operation. Mr. Cameron – then in charge of the blending department – began a series of experiments by vatting all the malts in the first instance and allowing them to lie for three or four months before re-vatting along with the primary grains to arrive at the proprietary blend. The result was such as to justify him, later on, in vatting the grains in similar manner".

This is how it stands today: you 'vat' malts and grains individually – and can offer them for sale as 'vatted malts/ grains', sometimes described as 'pure malts/grains' – but if you mix the two the process is called 'blending'.

Blenders – yes, 'blenders', not 'vatters' – say it is more difficult to produce a successful vatted malt than to make a blend. This is because of the key role that grain whisky plays in harmonizing and pulling together the individual flavours of the constituent malts. Ian Grieve, Bell's former master blender, used to compare the blending process with creating an oil painting, where the grain whiskies provide the white, sized canvass and the malts are the colours which after being mixed on the palette, are painted into the ground of the work to create a satisfying whole.

When you are making a vatted malt, you do not have the benefit of the 'ground'. Furthermore, and to continue the allusion, if you mix too many malts together you get – as with paint – a muddy brown mess. Those of you who have tasted *Chivas Century* (a vatting of 100 malts) will know what I mean.

Generally, vatted malts have had a bad press, which must account for there being so few around, compared with both blends and single malts. They are neither fish nor fowl: usually priced at the level of de luxe blends, but lacking the satisfying magic that a good blend provides; cheaper than a single malt, but lacking the complexity and character.

Having said that, some are very good. *Islay Mist* has been around for decades and might be said to have paved the way for the appreciation of smoky whisky. Gordon & Macphail produce a series of four vatted malts, each of which is designed to display the classic features of the regions Islay, Orkney, Lowland and 'Strathspey'. *Johnnie Walker Green Label* (actually it is a kind of greeny-grey), employs five Top Class Speysides, plus a dash of Clynelish and Royal Brackla and is a very decent dram. And the most successful of all at the moment, *The Famous Grouse Vintage Malt*, launched in 2000, has done phenomenally well – and justifiably so. In this case their master blender, John Ramsay, chooses casks at 10-12 years old from Highland's distilleries (Macallan, Highland Park, Glen Rothes, Tamdhu, Bunnahabhain and Glengoyne) and creates a slightly different vatting each year.

The first advertisement to add 'The Famous' to 'Grouse',
which appeared in 1897

Washbacks and receivers at Lagavulin Distillery.

NOTES TO
A CELLAR BOOK 1920

I used to endeavour to supply my cask with, and to keep independent jars of, the following: Clyne Lish, Smith's Glenlivet, Glen Grant, Talisker, and one of the Islay brands – Lagavulin, Ardbeg, Caol Isla, etc. The picturesquely named 'Long John', otherwise Ben Nevis, is less definite in flavour than any of these, but blends very well. Glendronach, an Aberdeenshire whisky, of which I did not think much forty years ago, improved greatly later; and I used to try both these in my cask. But I always kept separate supplies of all, and amused myself with these, alone or variously blended, at intervals. A friend of mine from Oxford days, now dead, held some mixed Clyne Lish and Glenlivet of mine to be the best whisky he had ever drunk.

GEORGE SAINTSBURY, 1920

George Saintsbury (1845–1933) is often described as 'the first oenophile', although he considered his seminal and delightful *Notes to a Cellar Book* (published in his seventy-fifth year) as 'very personal... so very little a book'.

This is not surprising from the author of the monumental *History of Criticism*, *History of English Prosody* and *History of the French Novel*; a man described in his *Times* obituary as 'cast in a mightier mould than most professors and students of literature... who had read and remembered everything worth reading'.

His study of whisky began in 1875, and was deepened when he was appointed regius professor of rhetoric in the University of Edinburgh in 1895, a position he held until 1915. Malt whisky was his passion; grain whisky he described as 'only good for blending, and for mere drinkers for drunkee'. Elsewhere, he remarks on how whiskies had changed over forty-five years, one of the very few descriptions of taste that has survived: 'The older whiskies were darker in colour, from being kept in golden sherry or Madeira casks, rather sweeter in taste, and rather heavier in texture; the newer are "lighter" in both the first and the last respect, and much drier in taste.'

THE WOOD MAKES THE WHISKY

*The transformation of new spirit into mature
whisky is as miraculous as the change from
caterpillar to butterfly.
The chrysalis is the oak cask.*

Dr Jim Swan

Of all the factors that influence the flavour of Scotch whisky, the cask in which the whisky matures is probably the most potent. While the cask cannot make good a badly made whisky, it can certainly make a good whisky great. On the other hand, defective or exhausted casks can also make good whisky pretty nasty. As the 'good old boys' in the whisky trade used to say: 'The wood makes the whisky.'

If you think about it, this makes perfect sense. It takes less than a week to produce a batch of (malt) spirit, from milling the malt to filling the cask; the spirit then lies in its cask for three or five or ten or twenty years...

The Mystic Oak

Once upon a time, new Scotch spirit could be filled into any kind of wood, but now only oak may be used: whisky cannot legally be called 'Scotch' unless it has been matured for a minimum of three years in 'oak casks of a capacity not exceeding 700 litres', and this in an excise warehouse in Scotland. (see 'What Is Whisky?' pages 16–25). Somewhat surprisingly, the requirement was only enshrined in law in 1988; previous definitions demanded only that the spirit be matured in 'wooden casks'. However, long before this time, oak was the wood of choice throughout the industry – although I am told that there may still be the occasional chestnut cask lurking in the murky depths of remote warehouses.

It is safe to suppose that, in the past, distillers would fill whatever wood came to hand, and the cheaper the better. Casks were merely containers in the days when whisky was drunk straight from the still. What's more, since wooden casks were the only vessels available for storing and transporting liquids of any kind, there were plenty of second-hand ones around. Wine barrels, rum puncheons, port pipes, beer barrels, brandy casks and sherry butts… all were cheerfully filled with whisky, whatever wood they were made from. However, most will have been made from oak grown in the great forests of central Europe, in Limousin or in Galicia (*Quercus robur*). English and Scottish oak, although also *Q. robur*, does not cooper well, so it was rarely used for making barrels. Today, ninety-five percent of the casks coming into the system arrive from the US and are made from American White Oak (*Q. alba*).

More Than Just a Tub

As soon as the benefits of maturation were discovered (in other words, as soon as it was realized that the cask is more than just a container) came the discovery, first, that oak does a better job than all other woods and second, that second-hand casks produce better Scotch than new casks.

Why Should This Be?

Scientific understanding of the chemistry of oak wood and of what is happening during maturation is relatively new, simply because, before the 1970s, the scientific techniques for exploring such matters were unavailable. Big advances were made in the late 1970s by Strathclyde University, Pentlands Scotch Whisky Research, and the Distillers Company Limited, and this knowledge began to be applied in the 1990s. Yet there are still areas which remain mysterious.

Chemists now talk about 'cask activity', and believe the wood performs three crucial functions, described as 'subtractive', 'additive', and 'interactive'.

Subtractive Mechanisms

In order to be bent into a barrel shape, the staves must be heated. Heat performs the vital function of altering the chemical structure of the inside surface of the cask. Without heating, the spirit will not mature; it will instead merely acquire a 'green', woody note. European casks are 'toasted' to bend them into shape; American casks are flamed once they have been raised, so their inside walls are charred to the depth of about a millimetre.

The carbon char itself acts as an important 'purifier', removing immature characteristics and extracting certain compounds (principally sulphur-based molecules) from the new spirit. The capacity of carbon to do this is exploited by vodka distillers, and also by some Bourbon distillers, both of whom filter their spirits through beds of charcoal to increase their purity. Since European casks do not have a heavily charred interior, their subtractive activity is not as pronounced as American casks, which may account for the fact that mature whisky from such casks often has a sulphury aroma.

Additive Mechanisms

Oak is made from cellulose (which contributes nothing to maturation and no flavour), but it also contains hemicellulose (which caramelizes when heated, adding sweetness and colour), lignin (a long-chain polymer which, like hemicellulose, degrades when heated to produce vanilla and coconut flavours) and tannins (which produce astringency, fragrance, delicacy and colour).

As might be imagined, a brand-new cask is much more active than one that has been filled before, so much so that Scotch is never filled into fresh wood.[1] If it were, it would emerge after a few years tasting very like Bourbon (vanilla, oaky), and a very bitter Bourbon at that if the cask was European. So all casks used to mature Scotch whisky, both malt and grain, are 'second-hand': they have been used previously for maturing

Bourbon (mainly) or other spirits, sherry or other wines. The first time they are filled with Scotch they are called 'first-fill casks', thereafter they are called 'refills'[2].

The first time they are filled, there will be residues of the previous incumbent (Bourbon, sherry, etc) lurking in the walls of the cask. These leach out into the maturing whisky, adding winey notes to the spirit. After three or four fills (depending on the length of time they matured the first and second fills, and upon the chemistry of the individual staves), they lose their 'activity': their ability to mature their contents. They become mere vessels, and are termed 'exhausted' or 'spent'.

They can be rejuvenated, however, by being reamed out and reburnt, a process called 'de-char/re-char' in American casks and 'de-tartrate/re-toast' in European casks. This re-activates the layer of wood immediately beneath the charred/toasted walls of the cask, but it does not make the cask as good as new. Ex-sherry casks will sometimes then be refilled with sherry for a period of weeks or months, to imitate the effect of a first-fill cask. However, a rejuvenated cask will not mature its contents in the same way as a first-fill cask.

The most obvious 'additive mechanisms' are in relation to colour: European oak, being more tannic, lends its contents a deeper hue than American wood. The degree of colour depends upon how often the cask has been filled (see 'The Amber Glass', page 220), but as a general guide, European wood hue runs from 'old polished oak' to 'young mahogany' (old oloroso to amontillado sherry, to put it another way; but beware of thinking the colour comes from the first incumbent), while American wood hue is all gold: 9ct through to 18ct (pale straw to deep amber).

Interactive Mechanisms

Oak is semiporous, which allows the contents of an oak cask to 'breathe' and interact with the air outside. This leads to oxidation, which removes harshness, increases fruitiness and enhances complexity. The interaction between the wood and the atmosphere is the least understood of the mechanisms of maturation – and, some would say, the most important.

It is this aspect of maturation that is most affected by the microclimate of the warehouse in which the cask rests during maturation. Heat, humidity and atmospheric pressure all play a part. Most warehouses are cool and damp, even in the summer months, and these conditions are ideal. In a hot, dry warehouse, the cask will lose water vapour, so the overall volume will go

HIGHLAND WHISKY.

THE SUBSCRIBERS have just received from the North a few casks REAL GLENLIVIT, bought at an Excise sale in Aberdeenshire.

They have also on hand an extensive Stock of FOREIGN SPIRITS, WINES, and TEAS, of finest quality and flavour, all of which will be sold genuine, and at reasonable prices.

ANDW. USHER & COMPANY,
44, Lothian Street.

A classified advertisement for A Usher & Co as featured in
The Edinburgh Star *on April 3, 1821*

down, while the strength remains relatively high. In a damp, cold warehouse (especially where the cask is racked close to the ground), the opposite happens: volume remains high, but strength declines more quickly. H M Customs & Excise allow for two percent of the volume of the cask to evaporate every year. This is called 'The Angels' Share', and amounts to around fifty litres over ten years.

Attractive though the thought may be, it is unlikely that extraneous factors like salt-spray, seaweed smells or adjacent plant life (heather, bog myrtle) play any part in the flavour of the mature spirit.

How the Casks Have Changed

Until 1946, almost all the oak used by the Scotch whisky trade was European, and many of these casks had originally contained sherry, which was shipped in bulk (i.e. in cask) and bottled by the shipper in the UK. The desirability of sherry as a first incumbent is recorded as early as the 1860s, but as sherry's popularity declined, fewer such casks were available to the whisky industry. However, since all but a tiny amount of the whisky made went into blends until the 1980s, the crucial influence of individual casks upon the flavour of the mature whisky was ignored, and casks were filled time and again until the wood was thoroughly exhausted.

The availability of European oak ex-sherry casks was dealt a further blow in 1983, when the practice of shipping in bulk was prohibited by the European Economic Community, which made ex-sherry casks very expensive – around five times as expensive as ex-Bourbon casks. Whisky companies that want European casks now have to buy their wood 'on the tree', have it staved and coopered in Spain, and make special arrangements with Spanish *bodegas* (wineries) to have them 'seasoned' with sherry before they are shipped. Currently, only around five percent of the wood coming into the system is European oak.

The vast increase in production of Scotch whisky since the Second World War has been made possible by the availability of American oak: ex-Bourbon barrels. These were almost unknown pre-1946, and their availability in large numbers since that date is simply explained. Shortly before the outbreak of the war (I think it was 1936), the American coopers' unions brokered a deal with the US distillers that whiskey must be filled into new wood if it was to be described as 'Bourbon', 'rye', etc.

The massive increase in international demand for Scotch was mirrored by a demand for American whiskey, so there were plenty of ex-Bourbon barrels available to the Scotch distillers. And they came cheap (although the price today is substantially greater).

Bourbon is matured in barrels holding around 200 litres. Some are shipped as such, and are termed 'American Standard Barrels' (ASBs). To save space on the ships transporting them, most are broken down into staves and labelled, and arrive in bundles called 'shooks'. In Scotland, they are reassembled in a slightly larger format (250 litres, by cannibalizing one barrel in three) as 're-made hogsheads'.

The Influence on Flavour

As I have said, European oak casks add and subtract different flavours from American oak casks. The latter are higher in vanillin (sweet toffee, coconut notes) and lower in tannin (fruity, complex, astringent notes) than the former. Also, since American oak casks are charred, rather than toasted, they extract more sulphur compounds. And finally, since European casks are typically twice as big as American casks, they last longer and mature their contents more slowly: the smaller the cask, the greater the surface area exposed to the spirit, the more rapid the maturation.

In short, and notwithstanding the fact than most whisky matured before the war will have been filled into less active (i.e. refill) casks, 'the whisky of the old days' was darker in colour, richer and drier to taste, more fragrant of scented wood (sandalwood, cedar), and often infused with sulphur notes. These deductions are confirmed by nosing and tasting old whiskies. Yet they are not necessarily better than the whiskies of our times. Many connoisseurs would argue that American white oak is the perfect vehicle for maturing Scotch whisky – fresher, sweeter, lighter – and I have tasted many examples which would support this argument.

[1] The only exception to this that I am aware of is Glenfiddich's Solera Reserve, where a tiny proportion of the casks which go into the '*solera* vat' are filled new.

[2] Some companies refer to 'second-fill' or even 'third-fill'.

CASK CAPACITIES

CASK TYPE	GALLONS	LITRES
Gorda *Also called 'bodega butt'; rare*	130	600
Butt	110	500
Puncheon	110–120	500–545
Hogshead *Also called 're-made hogshead'* *or 'dump hogshead'*	55	250
Barrel *Also called* *'American Standard Barrel'*	40	200
Quarter *Also called 'firkin'*	9–10	45–80
Anker *Archaic*	8–10	c.40
Octave *Archaic*	5	22.5

Some of the 6,000 casks of A Usher & Co, August 1890 – at the time, the largest bonded warehouse in the world

FINISHING TOUCHES

In recent years it has become common to adjust the flavour of mature whisky by maturing it in one cask, then moving it to a different cask for the final months or years. This is called 'wood finishing'.

"I'd rather my whisky tasted of whisky. If I wanted to taste wine, I'll buy that."

"It's not natural. Shouldn't be allowed."

"But what's wrong with it, if the final product tastes good? Anyway the punters love it..."

The topic in the Members' Room of the Scotch Malt Whisky Society is 'wood finishes' – a subject which can be guaranteed to get malt enthusiasts going. Sometimes called 'wine finishing' or 'double maturation', this is the process by which a whisky that has been matured in one kind of cask (usually a refill cask) is re-racked into another kind of cask (usually a first-fill or wine-treated cask) for the final months or years of its maturation.

During the extra months/years, the whisky rapidly takes on an additional layer of flavours. It has to be monitored carefully, since the second cask is by definition highly 'active' and can quite suddenly dominate the character of the spirit. I remember with a shudder a Bowmore, re-racked by the SMWS into a port pipe for too long: a horrible combination of perfume, smoke

OLD ORKNEY O O SPECIAL SCOTCH

Your luggage Sir!

STROMNESS DISTILLERY. ✦ ORKNEY. SCOTLAND.

Mc Connell's Whisky.

Pot Stills Only.

Estd. 1776.

Cromac Distillery, Belfast.

PER **3/6** BOTTLE

"Old Reading Abbey" Scotch & Irish Whisky

Thoroughly Matured & of Guaranteed Age.

REGISTERED TRADE MARK

Sole Proprietors
BUTLER & SONS. Reading.

CEMENT THE QUARREL. (Copyright.)

Published by John Dewar & Sons, Ltd., Perth, Scotland and London.

and sweet wine – which was nonetheless very popular with the membership!

The process is labour intensive, and therefore costly, but if properly done (and monitored) can produce excellent results - delectable drinks with complexity, balance and good flavour. Finishing also tends to 'round off' the taste and soften the mouthfeel, and this can lend a smooth blandness, rather in the style of run-of-the-mill New World wines: easy to drink, but lacking backbone.

Pioneers

The idea of re-racking from a tired cask into a more active one is not new – indeed, it is likely to have been a common practice in the whisky industry since the beginning - but it is only in the last decade or so that it has been commercially exploited.

Some say it was David Stewart, William Grant's Whisky Master, who first introduced a 'sherry finished' malt – Balvenie 'Classic' – in 1982/83, but this was not admitted on the label, so probably doesn't count. He followed it up with the hugely successful Balvenie DoubleWood (1993) and PortWood (1995).

Another pioneer was Jim Milne, Master Blender of J&B (then owned by Grand Met) and responsible for 'The Singleton', lanched in 1986. This was the brand name of the single malt from Auchroisk Distillery (opened 1974), and it was so named for the sound reason that nobody would be able to pronounce Auchroisk ('Athrusk'). Having matured his malt in refill hogsheads, Jim re-racked for a year into sherry butts. The result won many prizes soon after it was launched, but has now been discontinued. Like Balvenie Classic, it did not mention re-racking on the label.

The man who really put 'finishing' on the map was Neil McKerrow, former Managing Director of Macdonald & Muir (now Glenmorangie PLC).

Neil was fascinated by maturation and the effects of wood, and commissioned a lot of pioneering research into the subject. From a commercial perspective, being able to offer one or more styles from a single distillery increased Glenmorangie's product range. The first expression to apply the technique (although, like Balvenie Classic, it did not declare it) was the 18 Years Old released in 1992, for which one-third of the casks vatted were re-racked into sherrywood for the final two or three years of maturation. This was soon followed by 'Portwood', 'Sherrywood' and 'Madeira Finish' (all still available) and then a slew of exotics, some of which had been re-racked before 1990 (see page 165) – which goes to show the company's early commitment to finishing.

All these whiskies are well made and carefully finished, although some are more memorable than others – I have joyous memories of the Tain L'Hermitage 1975 and 1978, the Côte de Nuits 25YO and the Sauternes 1981; no memory at all of some of the others.

Me-Toos

Glenmorangie's sister distillery, Glen Moray, entered the market with Chardonnay and Chablis finishes. Diageo (it was IDV in those days) launched wine-finished expressions of their Classic Six (Glenkinchie, Dalwhinnie, Cragganmore, Oban, Talisker and

Lagavulin) in 1998: these 'Distillers' Editions' are still available. Morrison Bowmore introduced the successful Auchentoshan Three Wood in 1999, and followed on with Bowmore Dawn (Bordeaux finish) and Dusk (Port finish) in 2003. Glenfiddich went so far as to finish in casks which had formerly contained smoky Islay malts, to produce a dram which they named 'Caoran' (the Gaelic for an ember of peat); the same trick was used by Grouse for their Famous blend.

There were some disasters, especially among independent bottlings, but by and large consumers love finishes. Indeed, in some cases – notably the Classic Malts Distillers' Edition – brand owners were persuaded to release them only under duress. Following Glenmorangie's lead, the phenomenon has been largely consumer driven.

Pro and Con

Wood finishing is no substitute for good maturation. You can't take a young malt from a duff cask and expect it to cover itself in glory after a year in a port pipe.

"To finish well, you've got to start with whisky which has benefited from enough time in the cask to interact with wood and develop the fine, ethereal, aged characteristics of maturity. Maturation cannot be rushed", says John Glaser, the guru behind that most innovative of companies, Compass Box. "Which is not to say that there may not be someone out there who will try to take three year-old, immature whisky and pile a lot of oak flavour into it to cover up the immaturity and try to make it saleable. A similar thing goes on in the wine business."

Compass Box launched a novel kind of 'finish' in September, which they call 'The Spice Tree'. In this case it is not wine that gives the finishing touches, but additional oak staves, suspended within the cask. They are made from the highest grade French sessile oak (*Quercus petrea*), slow-grown, air-dried for 24 months then heavily toasted.

'The Spice Tree' is a vatting of four malts at between 10 and 12 years old. Eighty percent of the blend is re-racked into these casks for a few months (the precise time varies according to the weather), and is then balanced with the remaining twenty percent.

"This is not really 'finishing', since no wine is involved," John continues. "It is 'secondary maturation', a technique common in the wine trade, and I am happy to admit that I have taken a page out of the wine-makers' book. What I am trying to do is add complementary layers of flavour to mature malt whisky, in order to enhance both it and the drinking experience.

"This is not a 'novelty'. I wanted to create a product that will appeal to knowledgeable enthusiasts and interested novices, based on the whisky's own merits. It's all to do with balance and integrity. Here is where good whiskies, especially 'finished' whiskies, are separated from bad."

The proof of the pudding is in the eating. 'Spice Tree' is a charming autumnal whisky, full of 'mists and mellow fruitfulness' – dried apricots and brambles, even a hint of strawberry juice over vanilla ice cream; rapeseed oil, and at last, in the finish, nutmeg and allspice. I poured myself another immediately!

THE GLENMORANGIE FINISHES
(★ currently available)

★ 18YO (first bottled 1992; one third of casks re-racked into sherrywood 1990)

★ Portwood 1975 (first bottled 1994; re-racked for 4 years)

★ Sherrywood (first bottled c.1996)

★ Madeira (first bottled c.1996)

Claret Wood (8 casks from 1976-79; re-racked 1989 into ex-Mouton Rothschild barrels)

Claret Wood 21YO (limited edition for Pallmall Partners)

Tain L'Hermitage 1975 (bottled 1995; re-racked 1990)

Fino Sherry N/A (distilled 1983; bottled 1998; re-racked 1996)

Malaga Wood 25YO (distilled c.1975; bottled c.2000; re-racked 1999)

Côte de Beaune 12YO (distilled c.1988; bottled 2000; re-racked 1998)

Côte de Nuits 25YO (distilled 1975; bottled 2000)

Distillery Manager's Choice (distilled 1987; bottled 2001; re-racked into a port pipe 1998)

Château de Mersault 12YO (distilled c.1990; bottled 2002)

Sauternes Wood 1981 (bottled 2002; re-racked 1990)

White Rum 18YO (distilled c.1984; bottled 2002)

Golden Rum 12YO (distilled c.1990; bottled 2003)

★ Burgundy Wood (bottled from 2003 @ 10YO)

★ Claret Wood (bottled from 2003; limited edition)

★ Tain L'Hermitage 1975 (bottled 2003; re-racked 1999)

★ Sauternes Wood 15YO (distilled c.1990; bottled 2004)

★ Oloroso Cask 30YO (distilled 1972; bottled 2005; re-racked 1989)

CURRENTLY AVAILABLE 'FINISHED' MALTS
(not including Glenmorangie)
[See www.royalmilewhiskies.com – search 'finish']

Aberlour Sherry Finish 15YO

Arran Calvados Finish

Arran Cognac Finish

Auchentoshan Three Wood

Balvenie 12YO Doublewood

Balvenie 21YO Port Wood Finish

Benriach 1994 (peated portwood finish)

Benromach 22YO Port Finish

Benromach 21YO Tokaji Finish

Bowmore Dusk (Bordeaux finish)

Bowmore Dawn (Port finish)

Bowmore Sherry Finish

Cragganmore Distillers' Edition (Port finish)

Dalmore Matusalen Sherry Finish

Dalwhinnie Distillers' Edition (Oloroso finish)

Edradour 22YO Port Finish

Edradour SFTC (Bordeaux finish)

Edradour 1994 SFTC Burgundy Finish

Edradour 1994 SFTC Chardonnay Finish

Edradour 1994 SFTC Madeira Finish

Edradour 1994 SFTC Marsala Finish

Edradour 1994 SFTC Port Finish

Edradour 1994 SFTC Sauternes Finish

Glendronach 12YO Doublewood

Glenfiddich Caoran (Islay cask finish)

Glenfiddich Solera Reserve

Glengoyne Single Cask (claret finish, to celebrate the
  800th Anniversary of Ayr)

Glenkinchie Distillers Edition (Amontillado finish)

The Glenlivet French Oak Finish 12YO and 20YO

Glen Moray Chardonnay Mellowed

Glen Moray Wine Mellowed

Imperial 1990 Cognac Finish (Gordon & Macphail)

Imperial 1990 Sherry Finish (Gordon & Macphail)

Jura '1984' (sherry finish)

Ledaig Sherry Finish

Lagavulin Distillers' Edition (Pedro Ximinez finish)

Longrow Portwood

Longrow 1995 Tokaji Finish

Oban Distillers' Edition (Montilla Fino finish)

The Spice Tree (vatted malt; second maturation in sessile oak)

Talisker Distillers' Edition (Jerez Amoroso finish)

THE BROKEN GLASS

*On receiving the poet on the quarter deck, His
Majesty called for a bottle of Highland whisky, and
having drunk his health in this national liquor,
desired a glass to be filled for him. Sir Walter, after
draining his own bumper, made a request that the
King would condescend to bestow on him the glass
out of which he had just drunk his health; and this
being granted, the precious vessel was immediately
wrapped up and carefully deposited in what he
conceived to be the safest part of his dress.*

*So he returned with it to Castle Street, but on
reaching his house he found a guest established there
of a sort rather different from the usual visitors of the
time – the poet Crabbe. Scott entering, wet and
hurried, embraced the venerable man with brotherly
affection. The royal gift was forgotten – he sat down
beside Crabbe, and the glass was crushed to atoms.
His scream and gesture made his wife conclude that he
had sat down on a pair of scissors: but very little
harm had been done except the breaking of the glass
of which he alone had been thinking.*

JOHN GIBSON LOCKHART,
MEMOIRS OF THE LIFE OF SIR WALTER SCOTT
(EDINBURGH, 1837–38)

Elsewhere in his *Memoirs*, J G Lockhart (1794-1854), who was Scott's son-in-law, makes the interesting observation that Sir Walter 'could never tell Madeira from Sherry' and considered Port to be a 'physic'. 'In truth, he liked no wines except sparkling Champagne and claret; but even as to this last he was no connoisseur; and sincerely preferred a tumbler of whisky-toddy to the most precious "liquid ruby" that ever flowed in the cup of a prince.'

Along with John Wilson (see page 129), Lockhart edited *Blackwood's Magazine* between 1817, when they took it over, and 1825, when he went to London to edit *The Quarterly Review*. He was the author of several novels and biographies of Napoleon and Burns, as well as Scott.

'Squaring the Johnnie Walker Bottles', a cartoon drawn
by W. Heath Robinson.

JARS AND PIGS

There's whiskey in the jar…

Whisky only began to be sold in bottles when blending became widespread, after 1860, and even in the heady days of the 'Whisky Boom' of the 1890s more was sold 'in bulk' – by the cask or stoneware jar – than as 'cased goods': i.e. by the bottle (or case of bottles). Right up until the Second World War, advertisements for well-known brands such as *The Famous Grouse* still offered the whisky to private customers by the small cask, and you can still buy barrels (200 bulk litres) from Bruichladdich Distillery.

Early whisky casks had to be small enough to be transported on horseback or cart. They were generically called *ankers* – the word is Dutch, the term used throughout northern Europe – and held between eight and ten imperial gallons (thirty-six to forty-five litres). Larger casks were called hogsheads, a term first recorded in English in 1392, two years before the first written record of whisky-making in Scotland; these held around fifty gallons. The most common vessel for maturing whisky today is still the hogshead, now holding fifty-five gallons or 250 litres.

From the late eighteenth century, stoneware flagons or jars known as 'pigs' became a common method of purveying smaller quantities of whisky throughout Britain. Famous Scottish ones were Buchan of Portobello, near Edinburgh (which is still in business, and still makes whisky jars), Cochrane's, Govencraft,

Port Dundas and Grosvenor Potteries, all in Glasgow.

Spirits merchants, publicans, hotels and wealthier private customers bought by the cask or jar and either bottled or decanted the contents themselves (this was the job of the butler or 'bottler'), or, in the case of pubs and taverns, filled the whisky into decorative ceramic casks and glass dispensers.

Spirits merchants, and many public houses kept supplies of smaller jars, jugs and bottles of quart, pint and half-pint capacities, which they filled and dispensed to customers. They were returnable, a charge being levied by the owner and paid back when they were returned.

Both pigs and small jars were branded by their owners – whether retailer, wholesaler, blending house or distillery – sometimes lavishly, using a process pioneered in the 1860s by Port Dundas Pottery called 'underglaze transfer printing'. About the same time 'liquid glazing' was discovered, whereby biscuit-ware was dipped into a vitreous solution prior to kilning, giving rise to the familiar cream body and dark-brown lining and upper parts of many pots. Previously, pots were glazed by simply throwing salt onto the kiln fire, a technique known as 'salt glazing', which gave rise to an overall brown glaze.

Stoneware whisky jars remained popular until well into the twentieth century, particularly for exporting whisky overseas. They were durable, especially when sheathed in wicker baskets, which larger jars usually were; the owner's name or trademark could be incorporated into the glaze, avoiding the need for paper labels, which were easily lost or damaged; and they were not subject to duty as cased goods were in some markets.

Whisky jars are much sought after by collectors, especially those which are attractively transfer-printed or embossed, or rare editions to commemorate events such as the Great Reform Act of 1830 (known as 'Reform Flasks') or Queen Victoria's Jubilee. There are thriving bottle-collectors clubs in the UK, the US, Canada, Australia, New Zealand and South Africa.

'The very essence of human bliss – a glass o' whisky'.
A portrait (1782) by John Kay of Thomas Fraser, an Edinburgh
street cleaner, whom he described as a 'natural' (i.e. simpleton)

A ROYAL TOAST
Some royal encounters with Scotch whisky

"Did he drink it?"

We know that King James IV (reigned 1488-1513) ordered quantities of whisky/aqua vitae between 1494 and 1512 – there are sixteen references in the Exchequer Rolls, including, of course, the first ever mention of Scotch spirits – but what is not at all clear is whether he drank it, or used the stuff for medical purposes, or in connection with alchemy, or the making of gunpowder, or even as embalming fluid. As a Renaissance Prince, James IV was interested in all these subjects.

For the next three hundred-odd years, the royal accounts are silent in regard to whisky. The only royal connection I have come across – and now I cannot trace the reference (help, anyone?) – is with Louis XIV, *Le Roi Soleil* (1643-1715), who apparently enjoyed an occasional rissoli, made from imported Scotch grain spirit compounded with rose petals.

After an absence of almost two centuries, a royal foot was once more placed on Scottish soil on 13th August 1822. The foot belonged to King George IV (1820-1830), the place was the shore at Leith and the occasion was 'The King's Jaunt', a ten-day long royal pageant and 'plaided panorama' orchestrated by Sir Walter Scott.

On her father's instructions, Elizabeth Grant of Rothiemurchus raided her cellar to find 'pure Glenlivet whisky…mild as milk, and the true contraband *goût* in it' – illicit whisky, in other words – 'for the King drank none other', she recorded in her Diary.

When the King met Sir Walter on the quarter-deck of *The Royal George,* lying off the Port of Leith, he called for a bottle of Highland Whisky to drink the poet's health. Scott requested that he might keep the glass as a momento of the occasion, and stowed it away in the tail of his coat. Later in the day he sat on the glass and broke it!

The first distiller to be granted a Royal Warrant was Captain William Fraser of Brackla. *The London Morning Chronicle* of 20th January 1835 proudly announced: "BRACKLA – THE KING'S OWN WHISKY – His Majesty having been pleased to distinguish this 'by his Royal Command to supply his establishment' has placed this whisky first on the list of British Spirits". The King was William IV (1830-1837). The distillery has been named 'Royal' Brackla ever since.

William IV also bestowed his favour upon Glenury Distillery at Stonehaven, which stood fifteen miles south of Aberdeen, until it was closed in 1985 and demolished or turned into apartments in the 1990s. The distillery was founded in 1825 by Captain Robert Barclay of Ury, sometime Member of Parliament for Kincardineshire, and a distinguished athlete: in 1808 he became the first man in history to walk 1,000 miles in 1,000 successive hours. He was also an inveterate gambler, particularly on the outcome of prize fights, and spent much time in the south indulging this interest. The 'Royal' suffix was added in the early 1830s, owing to the good offices of a lady at court, a 'Mrs Windsor'. It is often assumed that this was the queen, Princess Adelaide of Saxe Meinengen, but we must remember that the Royal Family did not adopt the surname 'Windsor' until 1917.

The final whisky distillery with a royal prefix is Lochnagar. This came about on 12th September 1848 when, within days of taking up residence at Balmoral Castle, Queen Victoria (1837-1901), Prince Albert and their three eldest children paid a visit to their neighbour, John Begg, at his small distillery nearby. They were given a complete tour of 'the works' (Begg's word), and then offered a taste of the spirit "in its matured state…cleared that day from bond, which I thought was very fine". Even the children tasted it, and Her Majesty must have agreed with Mr Begg, for a Royal Warrant was granted a few days later.

Queen Victoria often drank whisky when she was in the Highlands, "neat, or in her tea, or with Apollinaris water…the astonished Gladstone once saw her lace a very respectable claret with some of Begg's best". She kept a bottle under the coachman's seat of her landau, "to provide stimulant to anyone who had an accident".

At the 150th anniversary dinner of the Pot-Still Malt Distillers Association in Elgin (1976), Prince Phillip made a speech in which he criticized Lochnagar for 'polluting the grounds of Balmoral'. Alex Macdonald, the DCL's Chief Accountant and a formidable figure, was incensed and, in a fit of pique, insisted that the 'Royal' be removed from all packaging and signage. It was only reinstated in the mid-1980s, with the Royal Household's permission!

Talking of the Royal Household, in the 1920s the Lord Chamberlain (head of the Household) invited a number of blenders to submit examples of their products which, if selected, would be used exclusively by the Household. The winner of the honour was James Buchanan & Company (already famous, and warranted, for its Black & White blend), but they immediately encountered a problem. The blend which was now for the exclusive use of the Royal Household (and which was immediately re-labelled *Royal Household*) was already being distributed, albeit in a small way, and the company was obliged to supply its current outlets.

A waiver was granted by the Lord Chamberlain, allowing the existing suppliers to continue to offer the blend, for as long as they, or their descendants owned their outlets. One of these suppliers was Jock McCallum, owner of a hotel in Stornoway, who had recently bought the ancient Rodel Hotel on Harris. He was allowed to transfer his licence to sell *Royal Household* to his new premises, and since his grandson still owns the Rodel Hotel, to my knowledge this is the only place in the U.K. where the brand may be obtained – apart, perhaps, from Buckingham Palace. It is delicious stuff. My brother and I and two friends had no difficulty drinking an entire bottle in ten minutes, prior to stepping over to the famous and ancient Rodel Church, where we were ushers at a wedding.

The only distilleries to hold Royal Warrants today are Lagavulin (first granted to the distillery's owner, White Horse

Distillers), Knockando (through Justerini & Brooks, the venerable London wine merchant) and Laphroaig (which holds a Warrant from the Prince of Wales, and is reputedly Prince Charles' favourite dram). J& B received its first Royal Warrant (as wine merchants) from George III (1760–1820), and have been 'By Royal Appointment' ever since.

Six blending houses also currently hold Royal Warrants: Johnnie Walker & Sons, John Dewar & Sons, William Sanderson & Son (*VAT 69*), Berry Bros. & Rudd (*Cutty Sark*), Hill Thomson & Co (*Queen Anne*) and Matthew Gloag & Sons (*The Famous Grouse*).

It would be indiscreet of me to say which members of the Royal Family are particularly partial to a drop of the cratur, although the late Princess Margaret was famously fond of *Bell's*. When I was last at Buckingham Palace, *The Famous Grouse* was being poured with gusto . . .

An advertisment from Punch *magazine in 1925 only weeks after John Walker & Sons Ltd had been bought by DCL.*

A ROYAL PICNIC

*Further, this Earl gard make such provision for the
King, and his Mother, and the Embassador, that they
had all manner of meats, drinks, and delicates that
were to be gotten, at that time, in all Scotland, either
in burgh or land; that is to say, all kinds of drink, as
ale, beer, wine, both white and claret, malvesy
muskadel, Hippocras aquavitae.*

ROBERT LINDESAY OF PITSCOTTIE, 1528/29

This is from an account of a hunt on the Braes of Atholl in either 1528 or 1529, which appears in *The Historie and Chronicles of Scotland* by Robert Lindesay of Pitscottie (1530–1590). The king was James V (1513–1542), the father of Mary Queen of Scots; the queen was Mary of Guise; and the (English) 'Embassador' was Lord William Howard.

The reference to whisky (*aquavitae*) is one of only a few known from the sixteenth century, and indicates the transition from it being a medicine or tonic to being drunk for convivial purposes. 'Hippocras' was also used as a medicinal drink, usually made of wine mixed with spices such as ginger, cinnamon and sugar strained through a 'Hippocrates sleeve' or sieve. Hippocrates is, of course, the 'Father of Medicine' and the patron of physicians.

WHISKY BOTTLES

Glass bottles began to be used for holding wines and spirits in the mid-seventeenth century, but they were very expensive, so only the wealthy could afford them. They were used mainly as 'serving bottles' or decanters, rather than 'binning bottles' for storing wine in the cellar.

Glass pads, impressed with the owner's mark or coat of arms, were attached to each bottle, and the bottles themselves were taken to be filled by the wine merchant, or filled in their owners' cellar by the butler (i.e. 'bottler'). Within only a decade or so, the middle classes were also able to afford glass bottles; Samuel Pepys records in his diary of 1663 that he 'went to the Mitre' to see wine put into his 'crested bottles'.

The earliest glass bottles had spherical bodies and long, parallel necks, with a rim at the top to hold down the string that kept the stopper in place. They are known as 'shaft and globe' bottles. By 1700, the neck had begun to taper and the body to become compressed into what are now known as 'onion bottles'. They continued to be treasured, and in Scotland were commonly used as decanters for whisky in public houses. In the Highlands it was traditional to give them as marriage gifts, crudely engraved with the names of bride and groom, the date of the nuptials and even with an illustration of the event.

Between 1700 and 1720, the onion shape was sometimes exaggerated, so the body became wider than the height. Then, about 1720, the sides began to be flattened by rolling on a steel plate while the glass was cooling – a process called 'marvering' – in order to be able to rack them in the 'bins' of the cellar.

Early marvered bottles were 'mallet-shaped', where the straight sides tapered away from the base. Over the next twenty years, however, they became taller and more cylindrical, particularly after 1740, by which time the value of maturing wine in the bottle was becoming generally recognized. By mid-century, many wine and spirit merchants had created their own bottles, with their name or trademark pressed into the glass pad, which could be returned for refilling with whatever liquor was available.

The classic French wine-bottle shapes familiar to us today had evolved by about 1800. There was a huge growth in the number of glass factories in Bordeaux, particularly, which was producing around two million bottles a year by 1790. Bottles from this period can often be identified by a slight swelling around the base, caused by the glass sagging while the bottle cooled in an upright position.

Until 1821, bottles were free-blown, which meant that capacities and dimensions were not standardized. So when one reads of hearty drinkers of the late eighteenth century downing three or four or even six bottles of wine at a sitting (this seems to have been especially common among Scottish judges of the period, who habitually drank claret while sitting in judgement), it might be supposed that the bottles of their time were smaller than those of today. Not so. Research done in the Ashmolean

Museum in Cambridge shows that the average bottle size was, if anything, slightly, larger than that of today.

In 1821, Henry Ricketts, a glass manufacturer in Bristol, patented a method of blowing bottles into three-piece moulds, which made it possible to standardize capacity and dimensions. Such moulds left seam marks (the way in which collectors identify them today), but during the 1850s, a process was developed to remove these by lining the mould with beeswax and sawdust, and turning the bottle as it was cooling.

Until about 1850, all wine and spirit bottles were made from so-called 'black' glass; in fact, it was very dark green or dark brown, owing to particles of iron in the sand used in the manufacturing process. Clear glass bottles and decanters were made, but they were taxed at eleven times the rate of black glass.

Indeed, because of the Glass Tax, which was first introduced in England in 1699, then reimposed in 1746, bottles remained expensive, and continued to be hoarded and re-used until after 1847, when duty on glass was abolished. The earliest known 'whisky bottles', such as a Macallan bottled by the local grocer in Craigellachie in 1841 (and reproduced in facsimile in 2003), were re-used wine bottles. Even after the duty had been lifted and clear glass began to be used more, whisky-makers continued to favour green glass bottles, often with glass seals on their shoulders. VAT 69 continues this style of bottle.

Many whisky companies continued to fill their wares into small casks and stoneware jars and offered them for sale in bulk. It was not until 1887 that Josiah Arnall and Howard Ashley patented the first bottle-blowing machine, and this invention allowed bottled whisky really to take off. In the trade, bottled whisky was termed 'cased goods', since it was sold by the twelve-bottle lot packed into stout wooden cases – like top-quality wine today.

Bottled whisky, properly stoppered and sealed, was less liable to adulteration or dilution by unscrupulous publicans and spirits merchants than whisky sold in bulk. During the 1890s, cased goods became the commonest way for whisky to be sold, particularly in the off-trade.

The use of plastic (polyethylene) bottles, developed during the 1960s and adopted by soft-drinks manufacturers, has largely been eschewed by the whisky industry, except for miniatures supplied to airlines. These bottles are called PETs – not a reference to their diminutive size, but to the material they are made from: polyethylene terephthalate. Their clear advantage is weight, and they began to become commonplace in the 1990s. Concerns about shelf-life and contamination by oxygen or carbon dioxide have been addressed since 1999 by coating the outside of each bottle with an epoxy-amine-based inhibiting barrier.

Bottle Capacities

As I have mentioned in relation to William Younger's examination of bottles from between 1660 and 1817 in the Ashmolean Museum, the capacity of wine (and therefore whisky) bottles remained relatively constant at around thirty fluid ounces during this period, in spite of bottles being free-blown. With the introduction of moulded bottles in the 1820s, however, it became much easier to standardize capacity, and this was soon fixed at 26⅔ fluid ounces (or one-sixteenth of a gallon, which is also equal to four-fifths of a US quart).

About 1900, this capacity was defined by law for a standard bottle, along with forty fluid ounces (equal to an imperial quart, or two pints), 13⅓ fluid ounces (half-bottle), 6⅔ fluid ounces (quarter bottle), 3⅕ fluid ounces (miniature). Brand-owners were not required to print the capacity on the label until after the Second World War, however, although some did. American capacities are slightly different. One US liquid pint = .832 imperial pint (twelve imperial fluid ounces). Whisky was commonly sold by the imperial quart (forty imperial fluid ounces) or by the 'reputed quart', four-fifths of a US quart or 26⅔ imperial fluid ounces.

Since January 1980 capacities have been expressed metrically on bottle labels, in line with the Système International d'Unités, when 26⅔ fluid ounces became 75cl, half bottles 37.5cl, quarter bottles 18.75cl and miniatures 5cl.

In 1992, the standard bottle size throughout the European Community was lowered to 70cl. The United States retains its (American) fluid ounces, with the 'reputed quart' remaining the standard bottle size (75cl). In Japan, both 75cl and 70cl bottles are acceptable.

GLASS: WHAT COLLECTORS ESTEEM

Age – free-blown and moulded (pre-1870) bottles have 'pontil marks' on their bases, created by the iron rod called a pontil, which was used to manipulate the molten glass.

Rarity – the fewer known examples, the more valuable the bottle will be.

Texture – variations in glass surface, number of bubbles in the glass, stretch marks, changes in colour.

Colour – unusual, dark or strong colours, or a colour which is rare for that kind of bottle.

Embossed – where bottles are embossed (uncommon in early whisky bottles), the clarity of the embossing, its heaviness (the heavier the better), its intricacy, and the interest of the design or words.

Shape – the aesthetic quality of some bottles.

Labels – any item with its original label, carton or box.

Contents – whisky collectors (as opposed to bottle collectors) are not interested in empty bottles!

AGAINST IT NONE CAN PREVAIL

It's a powerful solace for a man, the whisky...
Indeed it is a creature of infinite capacity...
There is nothing it cannot do. It warms the blood against
the chittering wind and refreshes you exhausted in the heat.
It can make you ill and yet it is a sovereign medicine in
sickness. It can exalt, so that a man sits with the so-called
immortals, careless of his kind, master for a time of his own
servile destiny. It can depress and humble him to crawl in the
excrement of his own miserable bowels of self-compassion. It
can sharpen a man's awareness of the world outside him and
of the specious prospects within him; and it can dull his
senses and his wits, equating him with the wormy clod
he is in fact. Without doubt it is an unpredictable,
multi-consequential intoxicant, imbuing its partakers with
manifold desires and proclivities: some to sleep and some to
bestir themselves; some to preach and some to blaspheme their
imagined creator; some to meditate and some to fornicate.
Much abused by its addicts and its traducers alike, it is a
complicated simple, the whisky, pure in essence but diverse in
effects; and against it none can prevail.

J P McCondach, 1983

The words opposite are spoken by the Reverend McAndrew, the sardonic central character of *The Channering Worm* (Canongate, 1983) by J P McCondach (1912-1997).

Jim McCondach was born and raised in Paisley, where he also spent his working life as a school-teacher, latterly as principal of English at Paisley Grammar School. As well as the splendid *Channering Worm* – which must have shocked his friends and colleagues – he published *Reflections in a Clouded Mirror* (a collection of poems), and *The Unwilling Jacobite* (1996), a novel based upon broadcasts he had made for the BBC.

CORKS AND CAPS

The discovery of a fifth-century jug with a cork stopper in the Agora at Athens shows that the virtues of cork were known to the ancients, but this stopper was not tight-fitting, and the use of cork for long-term storage vessels was apparently unknown to the Greeks and Romans.

Cork is the bark of a species of oak, *Quercus suber*, which grows in southern Europe and North Africa (principally Spain and Portugal). It is stripped from the tree every eight or ten years for around 150 years, its quality improving each time.

It was not until the end of the seventeenth century that corks began to be widely used in northern Europe; prior to that time, bottles were stoppered with plugs of wood wrapped with paper or fabric 'bung cloths'. The development of the tight-fitting cork stopper was a major breakthrough, since it permitted wine to mature in the bottle. The wine writer Hugh Johnson says simply that it is 'the most important event in the history of fine wine'. By at least 1693, it was known that corked bottles must be stored on their sides, so that the cork was kept moist and did not shrink.

Driven Corks

Corks which fitted flush with the top of the bottle's neck were impossible until the invention of the corkscrew, which happened about the same time as the invention of the cork in question. In the 1690s, they were called 'bottle-screws', but became 'corkscrews' by the mid-eighteenth century.

Being able to seal a bottle securely was of great importance to the whisky industry as well as to the wine trade, not because the whisky could mature – it doesn't. Unlike wine, whisky remains relatively constant in a sealed bottle. But cork made it possible for the whisky maker or blender to guarantee the contents of the bottle.

When whisky was sold in bulk (see 'Whisky Bottles', page 187), it was easy for unscrupulous bar staff or spirits merchants to dilute or adulterate it; in truth, customers could never be certain they were receiving what they asked for. Furthermore, once the contents of the bottle could be guaranteed, it became possible to brand it and then to market it around the world.

Stopper Corks

The flush-fitting, driven cork, usually covered with a lead-foil capsule, was the only method of closing a bottle until the invention in 1913 of the replaceable 'stopper' cork by William Manera Bergius of William Teacher & Sons, the Glasgow whisky blender. Bergius was the eponymous William Teacher's grandson and became managing director of the firm when it incorporated in 1923. Highland Cream, the company's leading brand, was then advertised as the 'self-opening bottle' with the slogan: 'Bury the Corkscrew'. To allay fears that bottles sealed with replaceable corks were easier to tamper with, the foil capsule used for driven corks was retained, often with a paper seal across it.

Screw-Caps

The next development was the screw-cap, originally made of aluminium, and sometimes of Bakelite, and pioneered by White Horse Distillers of Glasgow in 1926. The problem of tampering was addressed by fitting the usual foil capsule over the screw-cap, with a tape beneath it which tore open the capsule and revealed the cap. Such screw-caps were applied by hand, the bottle neck having a moulded glass thread.

A sales leaflet from White Horse announcing the invention summarizes its advantages:

No corkscrew will be required. The Capsule tears off in a flash. The Cap is easy and quick to unscrew. Freedom from cork taint is assured, and no broken cork can enter the bottle. The lined Cap is absolutely airtight and therefore the Whisky remains in perfect condition.

It is not surprising that White Horse was able to claim that sales of its whisky doubled in the six months following the screw-cap's introduction, although for a time the company continued to offer the blend with stopper corks as well, to satisfy more conservative customers.

THORNE'S
WHISKY.

"SCOTLANDS
PRIDE"

LIFE at HENDON or

Drawn and coloured by D. Jinkinson and dedicated, with permission.

PILOT'S FAREWELL

to John Walker Esq., distiller of Fine Whisky, Kilmarnock, Scotland

I was welcomed through the Empire by the e
And I've kept abreast of progress in the inte
To roads and farms and cities the bush has ğ
But the pioneering spirit is still strong in me

CHESTERS'

Fine Old Special

WHISKIES

"Who's been at my Whisky"

Lever Caps and Jigger Caps

The success of the screw-cap persuaded James Buchanan & Co, John Dewar & Sons and John Haig & Co to make a combined investigation into other available closures. The one they chose was the lever cap, made by the Kork-N-Seal Company, which was introduced for their brands by February 1928, and lasted for forty years. Barmaids called the lever-caps 'nail-breakers'!

In 1960, Whyte & Mackay of Glasgow introduced a larger plastic screw-cap called the 'jigger cap', which doubled as a measure or small cup. The company continued to use it for twenty-five years, and it was also adopted by Wm Teacher & Sons for its leading brand Highland Cream, between 1967-87.

Roll-on Pilfer-proof Caps

Also about 1960, a novel form of screw-cap was invented and quickly adopted by the whisky industry. It had the clumsy but self-explanatory name of 'Roll-On Pilfer-Proof' (ROPP), and remains the standard closure for blended whisky to this day. The manufacture of such caps was pioneered by United Closures and Plastics of Bridge of Allan, near Perth, which remains the primary supplier to the global spirits industry.[1]

The essential difference between the ROPP cap and the standard screw-cap is that the aluminium caps are issued to bottlers as blanks, their screw being created by machine on the bottling line. By doing this, it is possible to create a closure that has to be broken before the cap can be removed, the collar of the cap (an aluminium ring) being left around the neck of the bottle.

In spite of the obvious advantages of the ROPP, since the late 1980s the stopper cork has returned to favour, especially for malt whiskies and superior blends.

Detail from an eighteenth-century engraving parodying
Johnson and Boswell's 1773 Tour of the Hebrides

---

[1] I am grateful to George Thomson and Ian McGregor of Crown UCP (the successor to United Closures and Plastics) for information about the ROPP cap.

THE MYSTERIES OF BLENDING

The world-wide enthusiasm for single malts has tended to banish blended Scotch from the cupboard of the connoisseur. This is foolish: blended whisky is a miraculous creation.

Reputedly, it was Sam Bronfman, owner of the (recently dismembered) Canadian distilling giant, Seagram, who said: "Distilling is a science, and blending an art." Today, too many malt whisky enthusiasts look down their noses at blended whisky as if it were a poor relation to 'the real stuff' – as if malt whisky was the original and best style of Scotch and blend corrupted by the addition of grain whisky.

Having reminded such doubters that if it were not for blended whisky there would be no malt whisky - in spite of the prominence of single malts, around 96% of the malt whisky made goes into blends, and without this demand most malt whisky distilleries would close – I point out that blended whiskies are not better or worse than malts, they are different by design. The 'design' is the 'art' that Mr Sam referred to.

Another blender – I think it was Charles Mackinlay – famously said that the goal was to produce "something which is more than the sum of its parts". Dr Jim Beveridge, the current Master Blender of Johnnie Walker, expands upon this: "A good blend has 'gestalt', which means that it is 'an organised whole which is more than the sum of the parts into which it can be logically analysed'."

"For example," he goes on, "we use some very old malts in Johnnie Walker Blue Label – up to 60 years old – but the blend is not about simply 'being old'. We balance these old malts with younger grain whiskies (between 10 and 20 years old), otherwise their precious individual characteristics would be lost. The blend would also lose vitality.

"Likewise, some of the malts we use are very rare – either because there is not much around, or because the individual casks selected are superlative examples of the make – but, again, we don't use them simply for this reason, we use them because they each contribute to the gestalt.

"In order to allow individual contributions to impact on the blend, we use only a small number of constituents – around fifteen malts and grains. By contrast, Johnnie Walker Black Label employs over forty. So the personality of each of these old or rare whiskies works harmoniously with the others in creating the 'organised whole'.

"In a successful blended whisky you should not be able to taste any of the individual constituents; the important thing is the overall flavour – what we sensory chemists call 'the integrated flavour complex'.

"And this is where grain whisky comes in. Among other things (such as adding sweetness), it performs the key function of pulling together the flavours of the individual malts, balancing and integrating them into a homogeneous whole."

Blenders tend to divide their component malts into 'packers', 'core' (some call them 'heart' or 'base' malts) and 'top dressings'. 'Packers' bulk up the blend and interact well with the other components, but contribute little to overall flavour. 'Core malts' provide structure and overall character, and are usually drawn from distilleries that the blending company owns. 'Top dressings' are those whiskies which add a distinguishing 'top note' flavour to the blend.

A traditional blend is usually constructed around a mix of high-quality Speyside malts (making up around 50% of the malt component). Thereafter around 10% of Highland and Islay malts are added to 'dry out' the blend and add complexity (the smoky Islays rarely amount to more than .5% of the make up, or they will dominate the flavour). The remaining 40% of the malt components are 'packers', with low aromatic intensity.

Typically, the malt component in a traditional blend will amount to 30%-40%, and may require a large number of whiskies – Johnnie Walker Black Label typically uses around 40 malts, Ballantines around 55. Although, as Jim Beveridge says, successful blends can be made from a 'narrow palate', a smaller selection of malt components.

To the mixed malts is added the mixed grains. There are only six grain whisky distilleries in Scotland, so the choice is much more limited than that for malts (for which there are currently around ninety operating distilleries). But a curious fact is that although "many attempts have been made to create quality blends based on a single grain whisky, all have failed", according to Dr Jim Swan, a leading sensory chemist and consultant to the industry. In spite of the characteristics of Scotch grain whisky being much milder than Scotch malt, the products of each of our grain distilleries are subtly different and make different contributions to the blend.

In days gone by, some blenders made a virtue of returning the whisky to wood for six months or so once it had been mixed. This is called 'marrying', and it was believed that the various constituents need time to 'get to know one another' prior to being bottled. One blender, William Whitely, went even further, sending his marrying casks around the world before they were bottled. His bend was called 'King's Ransom' and was the most expensive whisky of its day! The only blender that I know of who still adheres to this practice is Tom Aitken, Master Blender of Dewars, for his premium blends.

⸺

Blenders sometimes compare what they are doing to composing or arranging a musical score. Jimmy Lang, retired Master Blender of Chivas Regal, explains: "The arranger will use his stringed instruments for melody, and the blender will use certain flavours such as fruity, floral, nutty, malty, fragrant, honied for his theme.

"The arranger will use the woodwind section for his harmonies, and the blender's harmonies will be flavours such as leafy, grassy, spicy. The arranger also has his brass section and percussion to complete the composition. This could be compared to the blender's flavours peaty, smoky, medicinal.

"Each arranger has in his own mind what his ear will hear as the finished symphony; so it is with the blender, as to how the finished blend will impart aroma and flavour. He has an idea in his mind what the finished product should taste like, and if it doesn't taste like that, he's got to go back and change a violin for a viola. Or a clarinet for an oboe."

You will have gathered from what these blenders say that they do not slavishly follow a set formula or recipe in reaching their goal – although the goal of consistency, ensuring that every new batch of whisky tastes the same as the last one, is fundamental to their job.

It is impossible to follow a set recipe for several reasons. Some of the malts may no longer be available, owing to the distillery having closed, or the individual malt being withdrawn by its owners to preserve stocks for bottling as a single (for example Glenmorangie, Lagavulin, Laphroaig, Cardhu and Ardbeg). Some fillings may not be available at the right age, owing to poor stock management or exceptional demand. Variations from cask to cask of the same whisky may have to be taken account of. Blenders get round this problem by finding substitutes – other malts or combinations of malts (say 70% of this one and 3% of that one) – which deliver the same effect to the blend. This is notoriously difficult to achieve, not least because the substitute malts may belong to another company, which needs them for its own blends. And since the required malts are usually acquired by exchanging casks, not by outright purchase, you have to have a malt which the other side wants. Here is Jimmy Lang again:

"We had a hell of a job at times trying to look for substitutions. We always had Strathisla Distillery, and then we built Glen Keith, but we did quite a bit of what we call 'reciprocal exchanges', where we'd swop Strathisla for Glenfarclas, or maybe for Aultmore or Cragganmore. Sometimes we had three-way switches. I remember one in particular. We had Glen Keith that was wanted by Invergordon; we wanted Aberlour and Aberlour wanted Invergordon grain whisky. So we arranged a three-way agreement."

How do you maintain consistency from batch to batch, and avoid what is known in the trade as 'flavour shift'? I put this question to Robert Hicks, until recently Master Blender for Ballantines and Teachers, asking him whether he compared the current batch with a standard reference from the last batch, or from one made ten years ago, to make sure they're the same.

He looked at me as if I was daft. "You must realise that this is impossible," he said. "The moment a bottle is opened, its contents begin to change, so your standard references are no longer standard. Their flavours have shifted! The only way you can do it is by holding the memory of the aroma and flavour in your mind and working towards that flavour profile."

If everything is running smoothly and the blender has the right stock of malts and grains to hand, at the right ages, in the right mix of cask styles (American and European oak), the blend can be put together without adjusting the recipe. But there is still the problem of faulty casks.

Maureen Robinson, who is responsible for quality control at Diageo, explained to me that before the casks are emptied (the correct term is 'disgorged'), the contents of each is checked for colour and clarity. If the whisky from a particular cask is much paler than its fellows, it may still be immature; if it is an odd colour or cloudy it may be contaminated, so the cask is pulled from the mix.

When it comes to putting together all the components, individual vattings (mixes of malts or grains, typically each of 30,000 litres) are all checked for off-notes – mustiness, sourness, sulphury notes, etc – and if found faulty, Maureen is notified and has to decide whether to adjust the blend or withdraw the entire vatting. Finally, when all the vattings have been blended together, samples are drawn, nosed and tasted, and compared with standard reference samples from the previous year.

Trevor Cowan, retired Master Blender at Mackinlays and Invergordon, told me about an occasion when a rogue cask was accidentally added to his blend:

"I was nosing samples in the blending hall as the casks were being disgorged and came upon one which was powerfully contaminated. Immediately I phoned down to the hall to tell them to pull the cask. Alas, it was too late: the cask had gone into the blending vat, and when I nosed the result, the off-note went right through the blend, even though the offensive compound was present in only a few parts per trillion!

"It was decided to try to lose the off-note by doubling up the vatting. Now we had maybe 100,000 litres of blended whisky – and although it was an acceptable drink, it was still not Mackinlays and had to be bottled under a different name!"

—

Master blenders are the wizards of the whisky industry. Not only are they responsible for developing new products, they must maintain the quality and consistency of the blends under their charge, while being constantly pressed by accountants and marketeers. Like master perfumers, some of them insure their noses for vast amounts of money – for without an ability to smell they cannot do their job.

Rightly, they are honoured by their employers. Some become international brand ambassadors and celebrities – Richard Paterson of Whyte & Mackay, for example, or Colin Scott of Chivas Bros. Others are more reluctant to seek the limelight – Jim Beveridge is one such, also David Stewart of William Grants, Tom Aitken of Dewars and John Ramsay of Edrington. All these men have been doing their jobs for over thirty years, and like the craftsmen they are, they are modest and self-effacing. Typically, Jim Beveridge plays down his role – and I am sure the other Masters would say the same:

"In truth, blending begins at the very start of the production process. If you don't get your new spirit right, you'll never be able to make a consistent blend. By the time the whisky reaches the blending vat, it's too late. So creating long-term blends, like the Johnnie Walker whiskies, which I am particularly involved with, draws upon the skills and experience of many more people than just those of the Master Blender."

BRANDING THE WATER OF LIFE

Until the late nineteenth century, there were few brands, and this was as true for whisky as for any other products. Retailers were supplied with goods in bulk; they weighed and measured them, packeted, poked, jarred and bottled, sometimes affixing their own labels, more often not. In some cases, retailers were supplied with labels by the producer of the goods, often with space for the retailer to overprint his own name.

Before 1847, glass was taxed (see 'Whisky Bottles', page 182), and clear glass was taxed at eleven times the rate of dark glass. Thus, bottles were precious and were hoarded. You took your own bottles to the wine merchant and had him fill them. Sometimes the bottles were embellished with your coat of arms or monogram in a glass seal on the shoulder.

Or you bought your wine or whisky by the small cask or earthenware jar and had your butler ('bottler') bottle it, or fill the decanters in the dining room. Whisky casks known as 'ankers' held eight to ten gallons; whisky jars, commonly called 'pigs', held from two pints to six gallons. You could still buy whisky like this in the 1950s.

Quality and Consistency

In the days of bulk sales, quality and consistency were in the hands of the retailer, and this led to widespread adulteration in shops catering to the lower end of the market (as a select committee reported in 1855). Dried mashed potatoes, plaster of paris or bone-dust was added to flour; horse-chestnut and sycamore leaves to tea; tallow and sheep's brains to butter, and so on. And with whisky, a pharmacopoeia of substances was used to disguise adulterated products, including 'sherry, shellac, tartaric and acetic acids, acetic ether, oil of wine, spirit of nitrous ether, glycerine and green tea', according to an investigation carried out in 1872 by the *North British Daily Mail*. Bottling, sealing and branding effectively took quality-control away from the retailer and gave it to the manufacturer – whether the product was whisky or soap powder, tea or jam.

Before you can 'brand', however, you must have a consistent and repeatable product. The brand-name acts in part as a guarantee that what you are buying has these qualities, wherever in the world you buy it. In relation to whisky, 'consistency' could only come about with the invention of vatted and blended whisky.

The reason for this is that every cask matures its contents in a slightly different way; each one is slightly different from the next, and even if it has been filled on the same day, the whisky each holds will be slightly (sometimes radically) different after three or five or ten years (see 'The Wood Makes the Whisky', page 148). In order for a single whisky to be the same, batch after batch, many casks must be vatted together to iron out any differences.

Early Blends

The first person to do this successfully on a large scale was Andrew Usher of Edinburgh, the agent for Glenlivet Highland malt whisky. An early notice in *The Edinburgh Star*, November 13, 1821, announces:

> Andrew Usher & Co respectfully inform their customers and the public that their stock of spirits, wines, etc., is at present very extensive, and that they are daily receiving supplies of fine Highland whisky. They have just now on hand a few ankers of Glenlivit [sic] which in point of quality cannot be surpassed.

By 1844, Ushers had developed its selling message and was advertising Glenlivet in London:

> The Real Glenlivet Whisky. Matured in the bonded warehouses in Scotland. This whisky produced in the district of Glenlivet, upon the estate of His Grace the Duke of Richmond, in the Northern Highlands, and pronounced by all connoisseurs to be by far the purest and finest spirit made in any part of these dominions, is now, for the first time, publicly introduced into London, under the patronage of his Grace… By his Grace's permission, the Ducal arms, on the seal and label, will distinguish the Real Glenlivet from all others. Price 21s per gallon for cash.

Ten years after this advertisement appeared (1853), Usher was vatting different casks and years of Glenlivet, in order to smooth out variations between one cask and the next, and to raise the quality of the whole by using some older whiskies. This was the first branded whisky: 'Usher's Old Vatted Glenlivet'. In 1860, following a change in the law which allowed the mixing of malt and grain whiskies before duty had to be paid, Usher (and others, such as Charles Mackinlay) began to produce 'blended whiskies'.

The mixing of whiskies from one distillery and another had long been practised by spirits dealers and publicans, but it had been done in a haphazard way, and mainly to 'cover' and add

The bonded warehouses of Glenlivet Distillery, 1887

flavour to the fiery and comparatively bland – but cheap – Lowland grain whiskies (or vice versa: to reduce the impact of pungent malt whiskies). But before long it was realized that blends had a much broader appeal than malts, and this made it possible to achieve a consistent product batch after batch – a product which could be branded. This was a very significant development in the history of Scotch.

Italian Warehousemen

Most of the great whisky houses started as grocers. Or perhaps 'delicatessens' is closer – 'Italian Warehouses' was their contemporary name – selling exotic imported goods such as tea and coffee as well as wine and spirits. Many learned the skills of blending from mixing teas, cordials and wines. The foundations of most of these houses were laid during the early decades of the nineteenth century, although the whisky side did not take off until the 1870s, with the second generation.

For example, John Walker's Italian Warehouse was established in Kilmarnock in 1820, but it was his son Alexander who developed the whisky side in the 1860s, and his grandsons Alex and George who turned Johnnie Walker into a global brand.

John Dewar walked from the family croft near Aberfeldy in 1828 to work for a relative in the wine and spirits trade in Perth; his sons created and built Dewar's White Label in the 1880s.

William Teacher opened his first liquor shop in Glasgow in 1830, and by the 1850s, he owned a chain of respectable 'dram shops' and was producing his own blends of whisky. His sons, William II and Adam, developed Teacher's Highland Cream in the 1870s.

Arthur Bell became a salesman for a wine merchant in Perth in 1840, and was sole partner by 1865. His sons A K and Robert only began to use their father's name on their leading brand, Bell's Extra Special, around 1900.

The blending side of these whisky businesses was stimulated during the 1870s by the fashion for all things Scottish (led by Queen Victoria), by the dramatic improvement in communications (which allowed them to export their goods to England and abroad) and by the vine-louse *Phylloxera vastatrix* (aka 'the devastator') which arrived from America in 1863 and, over the next twenty-five years, exterminated most of the vineyards of Europe.

By the mid-1870s, phylloxera had reached the Cognac region, and Cognac became expensive and difficult to get. Yet Cognac (with soda) was the drink of the English middle classes. By this time, blended whisky (with soda) was ready to replace it. The key problems confronting the emerging Scotch whisky 'industry' by 1880 were thus 'acceptability' and 'respectability'.

Acceptability

The opportunities presented by the new middle-class markets in England and overseas – starved of brandy or hankering for a taste of home – were immense. But the drink's historical association with rough Highland peasants, urban squalor, shebeens (unlicensed houses selling liquor) and drunkenness had to be overcome, as did its reputation for being 'hot and fiery', and having a 'bite' that was esteemed by aficionados but was not likely to appeal to those more used to brandy. In short, 'Whisky had hitherto been seen as a robust outdoor drink with perhaps some health-giving qualities, but it had an unfortunate association with the lower orders and therefore was quite unsuitable for the club or salon' (Colin McArthur).

The middle-class English sportsmen who had encountered whisky while on holiday in Scotland thought of it as an open-air drink, suitable for the hip-flask while stalking deer, shooting grouse or fishing for salmon, but certainly not to be admitted to the drawing room. As Winston Churchill, himself a great whisky enthusiast (Johnnie Walker Black Label was his brand), later recollected: 'My father would never have tasted Scotch, except on a moor or some other damp and dreary place. His generation drank brandy'.

Acceptability was closely linked to inconsistency. 'Londoners were often not sure what they were going to get when they ordered "Scotch", and when they got it they did not like it,'

Buchanan's Black & White Leads. The first colour advertisement for this popular brand, by Alfred Chantrey Corbould appeared in The Bystander, May 1912.

wrote James Buchanan, the pioneering whisky salesman and creator of Black & White.

'Scotch whisky of a drinkable sort was then a comparatively rare thing in England,' recollected the author Frank Boyd in 1920, 'and one still recalls the dreadful brass-cleaning concoctions which masqueraded under the style and name thereof.'

The solution, as these pioneering blenders recognized and acted upon, was to produce blends which were of higher quality and greater consistency, and more likely to appeal to the English palate: smoother, lighter, blander; the last, which would be deemed disparaging today, was considered to be a compliment and a selling point in the 1880s.

Respectability and Branding

The problem of respectability was addressed by branding, by advertising and by the tireless self-promotion of some of the leading figures in the whisky trade of the day, who loudly identified themselves (and their products) with 'High Society' and the mores of the English upper classes.

The most effective and commonest way of achieving respectability by branding was simply for the blender to put his name on the label. Often this was writ large, so that the brand-owner's name was synonymous with the brand.

In other cases, brand names identified themselves with Scotland: either specific places (not necessary factual) – such as Dew of Ben Nevis, Dew of the Western Isles, Strathdon, Lorne

Whisky, and the dozens of Glen This or Glen That – or with more general 'Scottishness' such as Johnnie Mac, Claymore, Roderick Dhu, Robbie Burns, Grand Old Ghillie, Spey Cast, Thistle, Scottish Arms, Highland Nectar, The Famous Grouse, and so on.

Such associations communicated on several levels. Grouse or Spey Cast, for example, made huntin'/ shootin'/fishin' associations that would appeal to sportsmen. Highland Queen or Scottish Arms spoke of 'heritage'. And for an age fluent in the works of Sir Walter Scott, and in which Sir James Barrie could remark that 'a Scots accent is as good as a testimonial', the very fact of

'Old Vatted Glenlivet Whisky' echoes Usher's famous 'OVG' – a famous brand in 1904, when this advertisement by Charles Lee appeared. Today, Masseys Brewery, Burnley, would probably be done for passing off!

identifying a product with Scotland implied integrity.

Associating your brand with royalty was another way of bestowing distinction – Royal Arms, Royal Liqueur Whisky, King George IV, Queen Victoria, Queen Anne. Also, since the laws relating to claims such as 'As Drunk by Royalty and the Nobility' were looser than they are now, gullible consumers might be reassured. Further reassurance could be had from the testimonials of city and county analysts, attesting the purity and healthy properties of the blend. These were often attached as back labels to bottles of Scotch. Another popular and increasingly important way of achieving the same goal was to display medals and awards won at international exhibitions, either on the label or in the advertising or both. The supreme testimonial, of course, was the award of a royal warrant: from the monarch, the Prince of Wales, a royal duke, or even a foreign royal household. These were proudly displayed wherever possible.

The purity, wholesomeness and age of the contents of the bottle were often emphasized in the description on the label. In the early 1880s, many brands were content with 'Scotch Whisky', but by the late 1890s adjectives were piled up to reassure and add value: 'Extra Special', 'Fine Old', 'Finest Selected Old', 'Old Vatted Highland', 'Specially Selected Old Highland', 'Very Old Rare Liqueur'. Such descriptions did not necessarily bear any relation to the quality of the whisky, and even today there are no hard and fast rules about what entitles a whisky to call itself 'De Luxe' – a French term, unknown in the 1890s – or to attach to itself any other kind of superlative.

Advertising

Early advertising capitalized on the association between Scotch and Scotland as much as branding did.

The prevailing idea was of Scotland as a mystic land of bens and glens, castles, clans and shaggy Highland cows – 'a delirious realm of the imagination in which the land itself, peopled by a noble race of bards, warriors and winsome lasses, exercised a magical, transformative sway over all who came there' (Murray Grigor).

Humour was often deployed, playing upon the popular stereotype of the Scot as a canny, parsimonious drunkard – albeit tough, brave and God-fearing. This image had been developed by *Punch* and other popular magazines since the 1860s and was enthusiastically adopted by the Scots themselves. Seventy-five percent of the jokes accepted from freelance contributors to *Punch* came from north of the Tweed.

King Edward's reign was also the age of Harry Lauder, the most popular comedian of the day, who built his act upon a grotesque parody of Scottishness. Although this might be an affront to contemporary Scots, we should bear in mind the millions of 'see you, Jimmy hats' we produce each a year, not all of which are sold to tourists.

More commonly deployed – and key to the idea of gaining respectability with middle-class English and colonial drinkers – was to identify Scotch as an upper-crust choice. Increasingly in the 1890s (and continuing up to the Second World War), many advertisements depicted whisky being enjoyed by gentlemen in their clubs, or at the races, or on the shooting field. Military themes were common, especially during the Boer War and the First World War, and usually involving officers. A bizarre poster from 1900 promoting 'W S Philips & Co (of Carmarthen, Dundee and Glasgow), proprietors of 'My Own Glenlivet Scotch Whisky' and 'Prince's Own Highland Whisky', depicts six senior generals (Baden-Powell, Kitchener, Buller, Kekewich, White and Field Marshal Lord Roberts) enjoying the whisky at a table overlooked by a portrait of Queen Victoria, with the Home Fleet at anchor in the background.

The kilted Scottish soldier was highly respected by all levels of British and colonial society, from the Queen-Empress downwards, and an image of him, as well as being wonderfully colourful and universally recognizable, communicated glamour, heroism, honour, steadfastness and tradition: a perfect combination of male virtues, and a message which said to the male target audience 'If you drink this Scotch, you'll be just like him'.

A further theme was tradition and heritage, applied both to the product and the blending house; like any parvenu who has made good, blended Scotch was eager to show a long and distinguished pedigree. Haig's was able to claim to be 'the oldest distillers in the world', thanks to the family's forebear having been found distilling on the sabbath in 1627. White Horse, or 'The Old Blended Whisky of the White Horse Cellar (Estab.

1742)' to give the full label description, claimed to be 'From the Original Recipe 1746'.

But the most successful of the lot was Dewar's. Its 'The Drink of Your Ancestors' campaign ran for years in magazines before it was turned into the first-ever film commercial for any product. In the print advertisements, an aristocratic gentleman in Highland evening dress (kilt, stiff shirt and white tie; the type has been splendidly described as 'that modern centaur who is a Scot from the waist down and an English gentleman from the waist up'!) is pouring a late-night dram of Dewar's Whisky, unaware that the portraits of his 'ancestors' hanging behind him (a Highland warrior, a red-coated, kilted soldier and an early eighteenth-century laird) have come to life and are eagerly reaching for the bottle in his hand. In the two-minute film, made in 1900, they climb out of their frames and dance crazily about in a parody of a reel, before climbing back into their pictures again.

In 1896, Dewar's acquired premises on the South Bank of the Thames, by Waterloo Bridge, which included a tall tower, formerly used for making lead shot (dropped molten from the tower to the river). By 1898, the tower had been embellished by the largest neon sign in the world: a Highlander, with his kilt blowing in the breeze, quaffing, day and night, glass after glass of Dewar's Whisky.

The Power of Branding

By 1900, three companies had emerged as the leaders in the whisky trade: Walker's, Dewar's and Buchanan's. Johnnie Walker & Sons was the leader in both the home and export markets; then, after 1904, it began to lose the lead, so that by 1908 both Dewar's and Buchanan's had overtaken it at home and abroad.

What did the Walker brothers, Alex and George, do? In 1908, they registered the brand name 'Johnnie Walker' and the following year commissioned Tom Browne, a well-known artist of the day, to come up with an image depicting 'Johnnie', their grandfather. Browne personified him as a striding Regency buck, complete with cane and monocle – unlike any citizen of Kilmarnock in 1820, but, we are assured by Alex Walker, based on a portrait of the old boy. At the same time, one of the directors of the company came up with the line 'Born 1820. Still going strong', and the company began to use both the image and the line in its advertising.

Next came the packaging. Walker had been filling into quirky, rectangular bottles with slanting labels since the 1870s. By 1909, the range of brands had been rationalized as Extra Special Old Highland Whisky, Special Old Highland Whisky and Old Highland Whisky. Now these were 'colour-coded' with black, red and white labels, and people began to ask for the whisky by the colour of the label.

Johnnie Walker, 'The Striding Man', was the first globally

recognized logotype, long before Coca-Cola, Shell or Mercedes Benz. Distinctive. Tasteful. Memorable. By 1910-11, Walker's sales showed 'an extraordinary increase', pushing the company back into the lead in both home and export markets.

A 1920 advertisement which advised Canadian drinkers that 'You must not drown Johnnie Walker' – i.e., by pouring on too much water

The Dewar's 'ancestors' campaign ran for years, capitalizing on the public's association between whisky and Scottish heritage. This ad dates from circa 1897

THE AMBER GLASS
Measuring Colour

The colour, hue or tint of whisky is measured by scientists with an instrument called a 'colourimeter'. The earliest colourimeter – and it remained in general use by the whisky industry until the late 1980s – was the 'Lovibond Tintometer'.

It is a simple affair. You load a test-tube sample of whisky into a light-box alongside a standard tint on a glass slide (or, more usually, a revolving disc of slides), look through a viewing tube and change the standard tint slides until you find one which matches the sample. Then you read off the number of the slide; they are traditionally calibrated on a scale of one to twenty (from light to dark).

The tintometer was invented in the 1860s by Joseph William Lovibond (1833–1918), but not manufactured by him until 1885, when he founded The Tintometer Company Limited, which still flourishes. He was born in Somerset and went to sea aged thirteen, took part briefly in the California gold rush, then returned to work in his father's brewery at Greenwich. His interest in colour began as a hobby; he was the first to realize that there were only three primary colours (red, yellow and blue) – not seven as was previously believed.

Lovibond developed his tintometer as a means of measuring quality in his father's brewery (which, in due course, he inherited), but he quickly adapted it to evaluating colour (and purity) in all kinds of other liquids and solids: oils, fats, tallow, dyes, blood, water… even leather, flour, fabrics, copper and steel. In a pamphlet he issued for the Royal Jubilee Exhibition, Manchester in 1887 he adds a charming footnote:

> The measurement of colour is so novel, and is developing in such unexpected directions, that the Inventor is prepared to entertain any new application of its usefulness.

Photometers

Lovibond's tintometer has mostly been replaced by instruments termed photometers that measure the light absorption of the whisky. A light beam is shone through the sample liquid and then through a filter which limits the range of wavelengths that emerge beyond it. The beam is then collected by a photo-electric cell, which generates a signal and a reading.

Colour Scales

Lovibond's scale was arbitrary. Tintometer Limited refers to a set of reference slides for the use of the whisky and beer industries as the Lovibond Series 52 (Brown) Scale. It has twenty-three glasses, running from pale gold to deep brown, calibrated one to twenty (three of the slides are fractions).

More recently, the Lovibond scale was replaced by the American Standard Beer Color scale (ASBC), and this has now been partly replaced in Europe by the EBC colour scale, developed by the Institute of Brewing and the European Brewing Convention. This has a range of two to twenty-seven visual units (unit one is colourless, and if a sample falls beyond twenty-seven – e.g. concentrates or syrups – it can be diluted), and uses a photometric method based upon the light absorbency of beer.

Somewhat confusingly, but based upon light absorption, whisky companies use their own scales – typically one to twenty, one to fifty, or one to 100 (from pale to dark) – and these vary from company to company.

Colour in Whisky

Classical viscimetrists (see 'Awakening the Serpent', page 231) discerned five 'cardinal hues' in whisky, termed 'Pellucid', 'Xanthic'; 'Rubious', 'Ambrous' and 'Umbrous'. Straight from the still, whisky is gin-clear (i.e. 'pellucid'); its colour comes from chemical compounds in the oak casks in which it matures. American White Oak casks (in which around ninety percent of whisky is matured) lend a 'xanthic' hue (*xanthos* means 'yellow' in ancient Greek), while European oak casks tend to lend a deeper, 'ambrous' (i.e. amber-like) or 'umbrous' (i.e. brown) hue to their contents. Rubious refers to the rosy hue derived from red wine barrels.

The casks are always 'second-hand', having first contained Bourbon or sherry, and sometimes rum or wine. The first time a cask is filled with whisky, the original incumbent may add a little of its own colour: for example, an oloroso sherry, port or red-wine cask may well add 'rubious' hues to the natural umbrous wood-tint. The more times a cask is filled with whisky, the less colour the wood will impart, even after many years.

So the degree of xanthic (or ambrous, rubious, etc) colour in a whisky tells you a great deal about the cask it has matured in: what kind of cask it has been drawn from (American/ European), how often that cask has been used (first-fill/refill), the approximate age of the whisky, whether it was finished in a wine cask, etc. Through this observation, we can anticipate its flavour: a key component of the enjoyment of malt whisky.

Because the colour varies from cask to cask, it should vary from batch to batch when the whisky is bottled. Yet it doesn't. To standardize colour differences from batch to batch, the whisky industry has long been accustomed (allowed by law) to adding small amounts of highly concentrated spirit caramel to the blending vat, typically around 1:2000 (.05 percent), although some cheaper blends may add considerably more.

The industry maintains that, at such low dilutions, it is odourless and tasteless. Much depends upon the character of the whisky to which the caramel colour has been added; pungent whiskies can take more, delicate whiskies less. But at higher concentrations, it is apparent, smelling of burnt sugar and bitter-sweet to taste. Yet some blenders maintain that it performs a key function in pulling together flavour in blends and improving smoothness and 'mouth-feel'.

Connoisseurs have long wondered about the addition of caramel. As long ago as 1969, Professor David Daiches, in his important book *Scotch Whisky*, wrote:

> I have seen a skilled tintometer operator carefully working out the amount of caramel colouring that goes into an eight-year-old (a very light colour, this), a twelve-year-old (somewhat darker) and a twenty-year-old (darker still) blend, colouring the whisky according to its age to fool the consumer into believing that the darker is the older. They say that the sweet, gooey caramel stuff that goes into the whisky is in too insignif-icant proportions to affect the taste, but in the case of the darker-coloured whiskies I am not so sure.

Describing Colour

The vocabulary used to describe the colour of whisky is imprecise and undefined – well beyond the accurate and objective remit of science. Since there are no rules, there is plenty of opportunity here to exercise the poetic imagination.

Metallic imagery is commonly used, for the simple reason that it communicates the lambent effulgence of whisky, often augmented by shades of amber. Unfortunately, we run out of appropriate metals about two-thirds of the way down the scale, Connoisseurs of wine will often draw comparisons with wines, or use the vocabulary of wine-tasting.

The descriptor is sometimes qualified by the addition of a secondary hue, usually referred to as 'lights' – as in 'pale gold with green lights'; 'polished copper with magenta lights' – and sometimes with other adjectives such as 'deep', 'mellow', 'dull', 'muted', 'lustrous', 'sparkling', 'brilliant', 'effulgent', etc.

*Dewar's White Label Whisky destined for the White Star Line,
circa 1910. Dewar's White Label was served aboard the Titanic
and the company's other great ships*

A VOCABULARY OF WHISKY COLOURS

LOVIBOND	CARDINAL	TINTS	METALS	'WINES'
TINT SCALE	*HUE*			
00	**PELLUCID**	–	Silver	Gin-clear
01	**XANTHIC**	Oyster	Tarnished Silver	Vin Gris
02		Bisque	Electrum	Manzanilla
03		Ecru	Talmi Gold	Champagne
04		Flax	Pale Gold	Soave
05		Gamboge	9ct Gold	White Burgundy
06		Jonquil	Yellow Gold	Chardonnay
07		Deep straw	18ct Gold	Eiswein
08		Maize	Old Gold	Sauternes
09	**RUBIOUS**	Solferino	Rose-gold	Rosé
10	**AMBROUS**	Fulvous	Burnished Copper	Amontillado
11		Topaz	Pale Amber	Old Sauternes
12		Saffron	Amber	Australian Muscat
13		Ochre	Deep Amber	Old Madeira
14		Henna	Deep Copper	Old Bordeaux
15	**UMBROUS**	Auburn	Tarnished Copper	Old Burgundy
16		Chestnut	Bronze	Old Amontillado
17		Mahogany	–	Dry Oloroso
18		Old Oak-	–	Old Brown Sherry
19		Dusky	–	Stout
20		Fulginous	–	Porter

THE QUAICH

There is no Q in Gaelic, so looking up the etymology of 'quaich' might have been difficult had we not remembered that, since Gaelic is a spoken language and spellings variable, we should go by the sound. There is no K in Gaelic, either, so we turn to C, and here we have it: '*cuach*: a wooden cup, a drinking cup'.

Interesting that the dictionary specifies 'wooden', since it is supposed that in earliest times scallop shells were a familiar drinking vessel, and that the wide, shallow bowl and lugs of the quaich were inspired by the humble scallop. Interesting, too, that the word 'quaich' was adopted throughout Scotland to describe this kind of vessel. Quaichs were not only found in the Highlands.

The earliest quaichs were carved from a single block of wood, but from an early date they were made from triangular concave staves or segments, held together with willow withies. It is impossible to tell how early, since wooden quaichs are themselves very difficult to date, but possibly as early as the making of barrels, which goes back to antiquity. More difficult to make than carved quaichs, 'staved quaichs' were often made from contrasting woods – 'plane for the light staves and laburnum, walnut or mahogany for the dark', according to that charming and scholarly authority, F Marian McNeill (*A Scots Cellar,* 1956) – and the fact that these woods did not grow in the

Highlands, indicates that rare and precious 'treen' was sought out for such items. Posh quaichs like this were commonly bound with silver, and before the end of the seventeenth century many quaichs were entirely made of that metal. The Royal Museum in Edinburgh has one dated 1685, and what is referred to as the 'classical period' for quaichs was between 1660 and 1710.

From an early date, quaichs had a sacral quality, being used as chalices, loving cups or cups of friendship. The late whisky writer, Gordon Brown, maintained that the two handles or lugs – the word literally means 'ears', and there are sometimes three of four of these on larger quaichs – 'symbolise the social bond of drinking and sharing, the cup having the means to be passed on in friendship and being received by the person beside you'. Rather like the pipe of peace of the native American. There was a tradition in a Highland regimental mess where I was once a guest – the regiment will remain nameless – to produce what was called 'The Doom Quaich' at the end of dinner, once two or three decanters of whisky and brandy had been polished off. The 'Doom Quaich' held two bottles of champagne and two of port. On top of everything else one had necessarily drunk, intoxication was rapid and assured!

The most famous 'great quaich' of recent years is that com-missioned by The Keepers of the Quaich – the world's most exclusive whisky club, founded in 1989 – made by Graham Stewart, Dunblane. One of the largest silver items made in recent years, it measures two feet across its handles and is decorated with ears of barley and Celtic beltwork. When new keepers are introduced they are given a small pewter replica in a drawstring bag, with which to drink 'The Great Toast' at the end of the Keepers' dinners at Blair Castle. At home, I use mine for serving salted peanuts.

The quaich has become the archetypal whisky cup, and as with so much else that is archetypically Scottish, Sir Walter Scott had a hand in it. According to his son-in-law and biographer, J G Lockhart, his custom was to serve 'a small libation of the genuine *mountain dew* [his italics], which he poured with his own hand…making use for the purpose of such a multifarious collection of ancient Highland *quaighs* as no Lowland sideboard but his was ever equipped with'. Predictably, Sir Walter himself drank from one which had 'travelled from Edinburgh to Derby in the canteen of Prince Charlie'.

Diageo has adopted the symbol of the quaich for their Classic Malts, and their excellent magazine for the Friends of the Classic Malts (which all members of the Society should become!) is *The Quaich*. The World Elephant Polo Association battles for the Chivas Regal Amateur Quaich Cup (I kid you not!). Canada's leading whisky club is *An Quaich*; and the leading whisky bar on Speyside is The Quaich Bar in the Craigellachie Hotel.

AWAKENING THE SERPENT
The Science of Viscimetry, now lost

I suppose all of us who enjoy the contemplation of whisky in a glass might pompously be called viscimetrists, although few of us are aware of it. What was once as important for sages as considering the movement of the heavenly bodies or examining the spilled innards of goats is now all but forgotten. I have even heard one chemist refer to viscimetry as a 'lost science... as little understood as hepatoscopy or xylomancy', but, like the latter (dowsing or divination by the use of rods) it had (indeed has) its uses, and its influence upon the minds of our forebears cannot be denied.

First, some definitions. Viscimation is what happens when two liquids of different viscosity mix, creating eddies and visible threads or ribbons. These are referred to as viscimetric whorls. The capacity of a liquid to create such whorls is termed its viscimetric potential or index. The study of the phenomenon is called viscimetry.

The essential difference between viscosity and viscimetry is that in the former the flow is continuous – a steady fluid motion of particles, where the motion at a fixed point is always constant – while the latter is irregular and generally flows in spirals. Semantically, the difference is that 'viscous' derives from the Latin *viscosus*, sticky (also *viscum*: bird-lime), while 'viscimetry' derives from the Greek, *ixos*: mistletoe.

Viscimetric effects are not observable where the liquids involved are immiscible (e.g. oil and water), and although some such liquids may be made miscible by the addition of an emulsifier (e.g. soap), viscimation does not take place. This only happens when the liquids have synergy.

The most commonly observed instance of viscimetry is when water is added to spirituous alcohol, especially whisky, where the colour makes the effect more observable. Since time immemorial, whisky-drinkers have referred to the phenomenon as 'awakening the serpent', and it seems likely that the Japanese expression 'killing the snake' (i.e. getting drunk) derives from the same source. Although apparent in white spirits, the whorls are less obvious, and with grape-based spirits the effect is more 'cloudy', even to the degree of 'false viscimation' or 'pseudo-viscimation'.

The same happens when a whisky has been heavily tinted with spirit caramel, the only additive allowed within the legal definition of Scotch, and added for cosmetic reasons, so there are no colour variations between one bottling and the next. But the fact that heavy tinting leads to pseudo-viscimation encourages some enthusiasts to limit their use of viscimetry to judging how much caramel has been added. A valid use, but something of a party trick.

The higher the strength of the spirit, the longer viscimation will be observed, but a spirit's viscimetric potential is also governed by its 'texture' and viscosity. So the familiar tests of 'beading' and 'swirling', both crude measures of strength and viscosity, fall within the science of viscimetry.

If the stoppered bottle is vigorously shaken, and the froth thus created lingers and forms small, silver bubbles (the 'beads') on the surface of the liquid, the spirit will have a high viscimetric potential. No beading occurs below about fifty percent ABV, and for the beads to linger longer than a few seconds, the whisky must have good texture.

Likewise, if it is swirled in the glass (which should be a snifter or spirits nosing glass), and if the 'legs' which trickle down the sides of the glass (also called 'tears' or 'church windows') run slow and thick, the spirit has a high potential. If they run fast and skinny, it has a low potential. Brandy-drinkers are especially fond of swirling, perhaps because the glasses in which brandy is traditionally served lend themselves better to the practice. I have heard it said that the viscimetric whorls revolve clockwise in the Northern Hemisphere and anticlockwise south of the equator, but I have been unable to check this.

For the ancients, the science of viscimetry was a manifestation of the mystic spiral observable throughout nature and discovered in megalithic and neolithic monuments on every continent. In Scotland, the spiral is at the heart of Celtic decoration and architecture: from megalithic stone balls, via cup-and-ring marks to the flowering of Pictish stone- and metalwork in the middle of the first millennium, and later embracing the illuminated manuscripts of Iona and the sculptural and metalworking schools which flourished on Islay during the Lordship of the Isles.

The relationship between viscimetric whorls and Celtic spirals is made clear by two further links. First, the root of viscimetry in *ixos*, 'mistletoe', the mystic plant which grew upon the sacred oak-tree, called *drus* in P-Celtic and giving rise to *druid* 'the servant of the oak', who cut the mistletoe with a golden sickle. Second, the colloquial (but ancient) reference to 'awakening the serpent' makes a linguistic association with 'the Serpent Paths' or 'Dragon Currents' (more commonly called ley lines), which connected the sacred sites and tombs erected by druids and their shamanic antecedents in the British Isles, and by priests from Crete to China, Polynesia to Hawaii, Africa to Australia.

It seems likely that the Romans were introduced to spiral decoration during the conquest of Gaul and Britain. So far as I am aware, there is no evidence that they understood the mysticism that lay behind the patterns, although there is a suggestion that viscimetric whorls were ranked among the auspices by the College of Augurs during the Augustan era and used for purposes of divination.

These connections suggest that the discovery of distilling, and thus the possibility of observing viscimetric whorls, might have been many centuries earlier than is generally thought. The problem is the lack of evidence from classical authors, all of whom are silent on the subject. But there again, if distilling and viscimetry were ranked among the 'occult' sciences, a veil of silence will have been drawn over them, as with other forms of augury, other so-called 'occult' practices.

Before we drink, we peer at the viscimetric whorls – evanescent and timeless as the aurora borealis – and wonder. Perhaps it takes the mind of a mystic to comprehend their full implication, and nobody has expressed this vision better than William Blake, himself a leading viscimetrist, in his poem 'Milton', subtitled, significantly, 'Thro' a Glass Darkly':

> The nature of infinity is this: That everything has its
> Own vortex, and when once a traveller thro' Eternity
> Has passed that Vortex, he perceives it roll backward behind
> His path, into a globe itself unfolding like a sun...
> Thus is the heaven a vortex pass'd already, and the earth
> A vortex not yet pass'd by the traveller through Eternity.

In the early twentieth century the Temperance movement and Prohibition in the United States gave rise to various strategic advertisements marketing the beneficial health and medicinal effects of whisky. During 1923 and 1924 King William IV Scots Whisky stressed quality and moderation. Sandy Macdonald, owned by Macdonald, Greenlees & Williams was another brand to emphasise that it was a 'safe' whisky, stating that 'Your doctor will confirm this if you send him a bottle'.

Mortlach Distillery, Dufftown, Banffshire, circa 1887

ROME WAS BUILT ON SEVEN HILLS, AND DUFFTOWN BUILT ON SEVEN STILLS

I knew one small town with seven distilleries and I knew an expert who could distinguish the seven by bouquet alone. These seven distilleries were in one mile of a Highland river; they used the same water, peat and malt, and the methods of brewing and distillation were identical, yet each spirit had its own individual bouquet. One, the best, mellowed perfectly in seven years; another, the least good, not a hundred yards away, was still liquid fire at the end of ten years.

MAURICE WALSH, 1950

Maurice Walsh (1891–1973) was an excise officer. He joined the service in 1901, and served all over Scotland, but particularly in distilleries on Speyside. Elsewhere in this memoir (which forms the introduction to J Marshall Robb's book *Scotch Whisky* (Edinburgh, 1950), he modestly writes that he cannot be called an expert, since he has only been acquainted with whisky for forty-nine years, 'and you need half a century at least to claim some knowledge'.

He was also a popular novelist, enjoying his first success with *The Key Above the Door* (1926), followed by many other romantic and humorous novels set in vividly described rural situations in Scotland and Ireland.

One of his short stories, *The Quiet Man*, became a cult movie (1950), starring John Wayne and Maureen O'Hara; another, *Trouble in the Glen* (1954), starred Orson Welles and Margaret Lockwood.

A ROSE BY ANY OTHER NAME

Most of those who wrote about whisky in the past say that the proper way to drink it is straight, or with a dash of water, or with a glass of water on the side. They repeat the tired old saw: 'Whisky is the only other thing a Scotsman likes naked.'

This is nonsense. You should enjoy whisky however you like: straight, with ice, soda, lemonade, Coke, ginger ale. But for a full and proper *appreciation* of the drink, there are certain guidelines.

While enjoyment is principally to do with taste and effect, appreciation engages all our senses: sight, smell, taste, touch (i.e. texture), even, some would say, hearing.[1] This is why, in the trade, the procedure is termed 'sensory evaluation' or 'organoleptic assessment'. But of the five senses, far and away the most important for assessing whisky is smell.

The Sense of Smell

Compared with sight and taste, our sense of smell is infinitely more sensitive.

• While there are only three primary colours (blue, red and yellow, from which we construct our entire visual universe) and four primary tastes (sweet, sour, salty and bitter; a fifth one, *umami*, a sweet/sour flavour associated with monosodium glutamate, is also sometimes accepted as a primary), it has been estimated that there are thirty-two primary aromas.

• While we are equipped with around 9,000 taste buds, we have between fifty and 100 million olfactory receptors.

• We can detect odours in minuscule amounts: commonly in parts per million, in some compounds in parts per billion, and in certain chemicals (some of them found in whisky) in parts per trillion. To grasp the enormity of this, it is useful to think in terms of time: one part per million is equal to 10.5 minutes in twenty years; one part per billion to 10.5 minutes in 20,000 years; and one part per trillion to 10.5 minutes in 20,000,000 years!

Congeners

The volatile, odour-bearing chemical compounds found in whisky (and other liquids) are called congeners (congenerics in America). Sensory scientists have identified over 300 in whisky, and they suspect there are as many again which have still to be isolated and described.[2]

It is these congeners that allow us to distinguish one whisky from another – and whisky from brandy or vodka or wine – yet they make up only .3 percent of the contents (the remainder being water and ethyl alcohol, both of which are odourless). This is equivalent to the depth of the meniscus in the neck of an unopened 70cl bottle. Vodka, a much purer (and therefore less aromatic) spirit than whisky, contains only .03 percent congeners, yet we can still distinguish one vodka from another by its smell.

Emotion and Description

Smell is collected by receptors in the olfactory epithelium, a mucous-covered patch above and behind the nose, which traps odour molecules and sends messages to the brain via the olfactory nerves. It is not known precisely how these receptors work, but the neural pathways from the olfactory epithelium connect directly to the lower brain without being mediated by other receptor cells (as with taste buds).

The lower brain was among the earliest parts of the brain to evolve, and includes the limbic system: the seat of our emotions. Perhaps this is why smell is the most evocative of our senses and the most closely related to memory.

Scents can bring feelings and images flooding back in vivid detail. The smells of childhood Christmases (the piney smell of the tree, raw and cooked Christmas cake, mince pies, spices, mulled wine, candles), the smells of school-days (floor polish, disinfectant, chalk, sweat, carbolic soap, sweets of all kinds), the smells of Guy Fawkes Night (fireworks, cordite, wood smoke), traditional household smells (cooking and baking, wax polish, cleaning products, coal or wood fires), smells associated with foreign holidays (markets and bazaars, foreign food, hot sand, tropical forests).

Barbecues and parties; flowers and perfumes; tobacco, car interiors, seaside smells, country smells, pleasant and unpleasant smells – even smells you have never smelled before. Among the many remarkable attributes of smell is that we can identify smells we have never encountered, although we may have difficulty in describing them.

Putting words to smells is often difficult and takes practice, but it is hugely rewarding, since the very attempt to isolate and identify an odour focuses the mind, raises awareness and stimulates appreciation. It is also an essential part of the fun of enjoying whisky (or wine) with friends.

There is no fixed whisky vocabulary – even less of one than there is for wine, which connoisseurs have been trying to describe for far longer. Yet the words used will tend to be dictated by the audience and the purpose of the communication, and arise from both objective and subjective analysis.

Objective Analysis

Objective analysis sets out to describe only 'what is there', limiting, as far as possible, the interpretive faculties of the person or panel doing the analysis. This is the kind of analysis done in the laboratories of whisky companies, and since the audience for such communications are colleagues, the vocabulary used is very limited and often derived from chemistry.

It is not necessarily descriptive; those with responsibility for assessing the quality and consistency of whisky need only to be certain that they are singing from the same hymn-sheet – not that their language means anything to outsiders. Thus, when

they describe a sample as 'grassy' or 'smoky', they must be
certain only that they all mean the same thing, even though
these descriptors might not be the words that immediately
spring to mind if outsiders are smelling the same samples. The
vocabulary varies slightly from company to company. As an
example, here is a list of the words used by Diageo's sensory
experts to describe the character of new-make spirit:

BUTYRIC

CLEAN

GRASSY

GREEN

FRUITY

MEATY

METALLIC

NUTTY

OILY

PERFUMED

PEATY

SPICY

SULPHURY

SWEET

VEGETABLE

WAXY

Subjective Analysis

Subjective analysis gives free rein to the experience, imagination and recollection of the individual, limited only by the opinion of the rest of the panel.

The language is descriptive and figurative; it abounds in similes (which compare one aroma with another: 'smells like old socks', 'reminiscent of petrol') and metaphors (where an aroma is described in terms of what it resembles, not what it actually is: 'wood-smoke and lavender' or 'distant bonfire on a weed-strewn beach').

It also makes use of abstract terms, such as smooth, clean, fresh, coarse, heavy, light, rich, mellow, young, etc, and these, usefully, give rise to contrasting pairs: 'smooth/rough', 'clean/dirty', 'fresh/stale', etc. But often abstract terms are relative ('smooth compared with what?') and sometimes double meanings are possible ('young' = immature; 'young' = supple, lithe, well-shaped). In general, abstract terms are useful for overall impressions – the general style and character of a whisky, its 'construction' and quality – rather than for describing specific aromas.

The language of subjective analysis can also be rhetorical – used to persuade or sell – but the effectiveness of the rhetoric depends upon the audience's understanding of the allusion. There is no point in describing a whisky as 'minty as a box of After-Eights' to a customer who is unfamiliar with these chocolates.

Chemical Foundations

Smells have an objective existence as volatile aroma-bearing molecules; they are not figments of our imagination. We are all similarly equipped to identify them, although some of us are more sensitive to certain aromas than others, and some suffer from a degree of 'odour blindness', called 'specific anosmia' (total anosmia is rare).

Our noses are the ultimate arbiters of quality in whisky, and although there are expensive scientific instruments available to help quality-control departments with their objective analyses,[3] no device has yet been invented which is as sensitive as the human nose. Sensory chemists acknowledge the supremacy of the nose, and sometimes think of it as a 'human instrument' which can be trained and calibrated. But the calibrations are of our own making when it comes to purely subjective analysis. The fact that scents are founded in chemistry provides a scientific basis for objective descriptors, but is also validates subjective descriptions and figurative language.

At its best, the language used to describe the aroma and flavour of whisky is both colourful and objective; at worst, it is marketing hyperbole, bearing little relationship to the product described. Increasingly, the tasting notes addressed to connoisseurs (such as members of the Scotch Malt Whisky Society), or to customers buying from reputable specialist retailers and independent bottlers, are detailed, accurate and helpful, while also being entertaining and appetizing.

Having said that, there is plenty of scope for the imagination when describing whisky, as the following two sections demonstrate.

Longmorn 1968
Le Bouquet De Soixante-Huit

While this whisky was being made, my friend McDowell was hurling rocks at the police.

Tearing up sets; manning *les barrières;* plotting in cafes. *'Sous les Pavées la Plage!'*– a slogan he was claiming to have invented by the time I joined him in Paris in the Fall of '68.

But my memory of this period is coloured by a girl in a library...

'A blond girl is bent over a poem. With a pencil sharp as a lancet she transfers the words to a blank page and changes them into strokes, accents, caesuras. The lament of a fallen poet now looks like a salamander eaten away by ants*'.

It embarrasses me to confess that in those days I wore a small bell on my desert boot. It made a cheerful tinkle as I walked, but irritated earnest readers in libraries - where I spent my days, in 1968, in Paris. It was her irritation at the tinkle which brought us together, that - and the fact she had a sore throat – which provided me with the excuse to suggest La Coupole, for coffee and something soothing.

On the way, we bought *un sachet de marrons chauds* (I was already half in love), and when we reached the café she wanted nothing but 'the linctus'. I can't remember what it was – Marsalla, maybe; perhaps Kirsch – and a compôt of prunes and figs. I ordered Spanish brandy, coffee and Black Bun. Later we drank Armagnac, which came with dark chocolates and soft fudge, and I had a cigar, still redolent of its cedar tube.

Then McDowell appeared, smelling of the barricades, spilled wine and that night-smell which is somewhere between moss and turned earth. New graves. He produced a slice of wedding cake wrapped in waxed paper from deep within his great-coat pocket. "Danny the Red's," he said as he offered it to us. It was three months old, but still had its marzipan.

'When we carried him away under machine-gun fire, I believed that his still warm body would be resurrected in the word, Now I as watch the death of the words, I know there is no limit to decay. All that will be left after us in the black earth will be scattered syllables. Accents over nothingness and dust*'.

* *Episode in a Library* by Zbigniew Herbert [Penguin, 1968]

[1] I know a distillery manager who can tell the difference between whisky which has been chill-filtered and non-chill-filtered whisky by the sound it makes as it pours. There is also the undeniable sensory pleasure of cracking open or drawing the cork of a new bottle!

[2] Coincidentally, it is reckoned that there are around 300 volatile odour-bearing compounds in human scent – a personal olfactory signature, picked up by sniffer dogs.

[3] These instruments are called gas chromatographs. They register smells by measuring the amounts of volatile compounds present in a sample and communicate the information graphically.

Bowmore 1993
Through The Looking Glass

We enter a white room, a tabula rasa – perhaps John Updike's white sheet of paper, "radiant as the sun rising in the morning", or Kandinski's freshly sized canvas, "pregnant with all possibility".

We find it unnerving, but not unduly ominous. We have been in similar rooms before. There is a profound silence here; the temperature is neither hot nor cold; the atmosphere, at least to begin with, is not oppressive, even when the door by which we have entered merges with the white wall. There are no windows, and although the room is bright, no immediately discernable source of light. An operating theatre comes to mind, and this sets going a butterfly-tremble in our guts.

Inevitably, our attention is focussed upon the glass which stands alone on a white table in the middle of the room. Mercifully, bearing no similarity to an operating table. It is a tulip glass, a bulbous copita, and contains what looks like vin gris – a pale liquid, the colour of tarnished silver shot with lime, glittering in the even light. Beside it is a flask of water.

We take up the glass and sniff. The physical sensation is both peppery and nettley. Then the visions begin…

The room is now a kitchen. On a formica dresser is an Arbroath smokie, half unwrapped from its waxed paper packet. A pan of gooseberries is bubbling on the stove. The sink is full of dirty dishes and very soapy hot water, and the scent from this mingles with a background of artificial air-freshener.

A large, raw-boned, somewhat ill-kempt woman in her thirties is cleaning a window with a cloth soaked in spirituous cleaning fluid which smells of vinyl and antiseptic. The cloth squeaks across the glass…

To clear the mirror, as it were, we take a sip from the copita. The flavour is very hot – at once fiery and spicy and etheric – Fisherman's Friend lozenges. Aggressively acidic and salty, with distant diesel fumes. We hastily add water.

Now we are observing a fishing boat, moored alongside a pier. The boat's diesel engine is running and puffing grey smoke. In a moment, we notice it is not only the engine that is making smoke: the woman we encountered earlier is now reducing seal blubber in a pot over a brazier, which she is stoking with bits of tyre and animal bones. She is wearing a Burberry baseball cap and a PVC apron. Fishing nets lie on the deck, with the dry remains of prawns and crabs entangled in them. Bladder-wrack clings to the pier, whispering.

Sea-weed imbues the flavour of the liquid – iodine and operating theatres; a taste which begins sweet, becomes acidic and salty; a texture at once oily and spritzich, as if the seaweed had been sprinkled with cayenne pepper. Smouldering tractor tyres still linger in the mouth, and our final vision is of a friendly, Burberry crowned face saying:

"Whit yoos want?"

Most whisky firms produced an annual price list, such as this one by
Chivas Brothers from 1891

Drinking the health of the Duke of Rothesay at the Festival of Highland Society, 1872

TASTE

'Why does whisky taste as it does?' and 'Has it always tasted like this?' are among the most engaging and oft-asked questions when two or more whisky enthusiasts are gathered together. I will attempt to explore them – to say 'answer' would be presumptuous – tangentially, by looking at how whisky was made in the past, and how this might have contributed to flavour. For the historical sources are mainly silent about what whisky tasted like, dwelling rather upon its effects.

Let us consider, first, the raw materials: cereals, malted so the starch in them can be transformed into sugar by hot water, and then into alcohol – a thin ale – by the action of yeast. Barley was the 'drink crop' in medieval Scotland, although there are very occasional references to oats (the staple 'food crop') being used for making whisky. The type of cereal is the first influence upon flavour, and poor quality raw materials make for inadequate concentration and fractionation, and taint the spirit with grainy flavours.

The kind of barley grown before the improvements of the Agricultural Revolution was bere – a coarse variety, poor quality and low yielding, and, it might be assumed, often producing coarse spirit. But not necessarily.

In 1994, Richard Paterson, Kyndal's Master Blender (formerly JBB, formerly Whyte & Mackay), distilled a mash from bere in the kind of primitive still that might have been used in the fifteenth century. The resulting spirit, he tells me, was very different from modern new make: very light in both strength and flavour; floral and lightly biscuity. But it was *clean*.

The process of distilling transforms the 'thin ale' into ethereal spirit. The ale itself, the 'wash', should be relatively clear and free of solids, or these will stick to the base of the still and impart a scorched flavour to the distillate. Rummagers – devices made of copper chain mail which rumble around the bottom of the still and help to prevent this – were invented at the end of the eighteenth century, but they were only used in large commercial stills, and these had other faults, as we shall see. Eighteenth-century travellers in Scotland often described the whisky they tasted as being 'empyreumatic', which my Chambers Dictionary defines as "the burned smell and acrid taste that come when animal or vegetable substances are burned". No wonder that most whisky was drunk as punch during the eighteenth century, flavoured with sugar, lemon and spices.

The purity of the spirit depends, to a large extent, upon the contact it has with copper. You cannot make whisky in stills and condensers fashioned from any other material, and you cannot make good whisky unless the size of your still and the way you run it allows for plenty of contact with the copper. During the late eighteenth century the tax regime encouraged commercial distillers in the Lowlands to use large stills with saucer-shaped bottoms, capable of being worked off in minutes. The resulting spirit, having had little contact with the copper sides of the still, will have been sulphurous and raw – another reason for disguising it in a punch. Even this was, on occasion, not too appetising: the night before the Battle of Prestonpans, 'Jupiter' Carlyle made a bowl of punch for his friends after dinner, "…and after one bottle of claret to wash away the taste of the whisky punch, we fell to the Burgundy…" At this time, and until the end of the eighteenth century, brandy and French wines were still the drink of choice for those who could afford them.

The same tax regime applied differently above the Highland Line, and licensed distillers here were able to distil more slowly, in smaller stills and from weaker washes, all of which contributed to Highland whisky having a higher reputation than that made in the Lowlands. Unlicensed distillers (i.e. smugglers) could make whisky as they pleased: some of it was very highly regarded (see Elizabeth Grant's comment below), but it is safe to assume that much of it was horrid.

Given the influence of copper, if you distil your spirit more than once, you will increase its purity as well as its strength. We know from Martin Martin (*Journey to the Western Isles*, 1695) that this was done in Lewis, so presumably it was done elsewhere: "[Their surplus of corn] disposed the Natives to brew several sorts of Liquors, as common *Usquebaugh*, another call'd *Trestarig, id est, Aqua-vitae*, three times distilled, which is strong and hot; a third sort is four-times distill'd, and this by the Natives is call'd *Usquebaugh-baul, id est Usquebaugh*, which at first taste affects all the Members of the Body: two spoonfuls of this Last Liquor is a sufficient dose; and if any Man exceed this, it would presently stop his Breath, and endanger his Life."

Let us move to maturation, the second great contributor to flavour – at least in modern whisky. Filling your new make spirit into an oak cask and leaving it for a period of time takes much of the fire out of it, mellows it, adds complexity. Filling into a 'good' cask performs miracles, which the good Dr Swan, Professor of the Society's 'Whisky School', describes as equivalent to the transformation of a caterpillar into a butterfly. Filling into a highly active cask (such as a new sherry butt) will replace the 'distillery character' with characteristics from the cask (e.g. sherry).

The first direct reference to the benefits of maturation that I have come across is in Elizabeth Grant of Rothiemurchus's *Diary* (1822), when she sends her best cask of whisky to her father in Edinburgh for the delectation of King George IV. She describes it as being "long in the wood...mild as milk, and the true contraband *goût* in it".

From the eighteenth century to the end of the nineteenth, any cask was used, but the benefits of oak-wood, and of ex-sherry casks in particular, were noted at least as early as the 1870s (by Thomas Sandeman of VAT 69, for example). Until 1946, 99% of the oak was European, whereas today 90% is American white oak. The different species give different flavours, the former generally being darker, fruitier and more tannic.

From all this we might conclude that whisky made even sixty years ago tasted different to that which is made today. But the differences are not great. Indeed, I have tasted Macallan made in 1874 and bottled at 16 years old and it bore a clear resemblance to Macallan today. In truth, if the whisky was well made and matured in good casks – as much of it was by the 1870s – I believe it will have tasted similar to today's whiskies and will have been of equal quality.

The Isle of Iona, where St Columba founded an abbey in the 6th century, and where for many centuries the kings of Scots were buried, is still a spiritual place. This advertisement, by Alfred Pearce, Arthur Buchanan and John Hall, was registered in November 1907

GOOD TASTE

I pass on to another kind of enemy, the men who drink whisky. With pain, and not without a hope that they may yet be saved, let us number their sins. Foremost among these is that they drink not for the pleasure of drinking nor for any merits of flavour or bouquet which the whisky may possess, but simply in order to obtain a certain physical effect. They regard whisky not as a beverage, but as a drug. Not as an end, but as a means to an end. It is, indeed, a heresy of the darker sort, doubly to be condemned in that it lends a sad, superficial plausibility to the sneers of the precious. Whisky suffers its worst insults at the hands of the swillers, the drinkers-to-get-drunk who have not organs of taste and smell in them but only gauges of alcoholic content, the boozers, the 'let's-have-a-spot' and 'make-it-a-quick-one' gentry, and all the rest who dwell in a darkness where there are no whiskies but only whisky – and, of course, soda.

…As a result there has been a tendency to abolish whisky from the table of the connoisseur to the saloon bar and the golf-club smoke-room. The notion that we can possibly develop a palate for whisky is guaranteed to produce a smile of derision in any company except that of a few Scottish lairds, farmers, gamekeepers, and bailies, relics of a vanished age of gold when the vintages of the north had their students and lovers.

AENEAS MACDONALD, *WHISKY* (EDINBURGH 1930)

Whisky is arguably the first ever book about its subject, written from the consumer's perspective: earlier studies had been technical, scientific or quasi-historical. But until this year (2006) nobody knew who 'Aeneas MacDonald' was.

Happily, the book has now been republished, with an introduction by the whisky writer and bibliophile Ian Buxton, in which he reveals that MacDonald was, in fact, George Malcolm Thomson (1899–1996) publisher, journalist and author of over twenty books.

But why the pseudonym? Well, first, George Thomson's family were ardent teetotallers, and he wished to avoid offending his mother. Second, he was one of the founders of the Porpoise Press, *Whisky*'s original publisher, and as he himself wrote: "I should hate to think the Press existed to publish me alone." Third, two years prior to publication, he had written a highly controversial book entitled *Caledonia, or the Future of the Scots*, which led to him being (in his own words) "the best-hated man in Scotland"! He did not want such opprobrium to blight his new book.

Whisky is the whisky book I would take to a desert island, were I obliged to take only one. Although small in size, it is huge in stature, and it is written with a depth of knowledge which is utterly reliable, a sense of humour and irony which at times makes one laugh out loud, and a fearlessness which verges on polemic. The contribution it makes to our appreciation of Scotch is as valid today as it was when he wrote it, and above all it lends comfort by reminding us how lucky we are to have so many whiskies – especially malt whiskies – to choose from today. "The age of gold", about which he wrote nostalgically, has returned, and now there is greater choice than ever before in history.

THE THREE STAGES OF INTOXICATION

Grades or measures of drunkenness are acknowledged and colourfully described in Scotland. Even our courts recognize the difference between one stage of intoxication and the next. Defences such as 'Ah, wiz fu, but no' that fu' or 'my client had taken only a slight refreshment' are familiar, and have succeeded. Indeed, in 1942, Lord Justice Clerk Cooper opined from the bench that 'the words "in a state of intoxication" *prima facie* suggest a condition graver and more extreme than that which is suggested by words such as "drunk" or "under the influence of drink", and it is desirable that that distinction should be kept clearly in view for the purposes of prosecutions based upon an alleged breach of [such] condition'.

The fullest and most colourful treatment of 'degrees of intoxication' I have come across is an unpublished memoir by one William Grant Stewart, who was brought up in a public house at Tomintoul on Speyside during the 1820s. Tomintoul is one of the highest villages in Scotland, and is well-known to listeners of BBC Radio 4 for invariably being the first to be cut off by snow drifts. I have been unable to find out anything about William Grant Stewart, but he supported his own recollections of life in the inn with the observations of one whom he describes as 'a late ingenious Highland physician', and this sage perceived three stages of drunkenness, which he described as 'Blythe', 'Bosky' and 'Borajo'.

'Under the influence of the first bottle, the Blythe stage of excitement begins with an increase of heat, muscular strength and accelerated circulation, animated countenance; vivid powers of imagination, and an easy flow of wit and humour... Daily cares are left behind... And now and anon is heard a Gaelic song.

As the drinking continues [with bottle number two], the party verges on intoxication. Repetition of toasts; the vacant laugh and incoherent exclamation, mingled with emphatic oaths, perpetually burst upon the ear of the auditory. Noise and ribaldry usurp the place of mirth. It is at this stage that quarrelling and fighting generally take place. Construing some casual remark as an insult, a violent collie-shangie or altercation ensues. This is the 'Bosky' stage...

[With bottle number three] all excessive excitement is followed by a corresponding collapse, the operators by degrees sink into a state of lethargy, or at best their exclamations are incoherent and confused, muttering unintelligible soliloquies; these subsiding efforts of the imagination soon subsiding into a state of profound somnolency, accompanied by snoring or stertorous sound. The drinker is now in the third or 'Borajo' state, or what is commonly called "dead drunk"'.

The words used by Mr Stewart's mentor to describe the three stages are interesting. 'Blythe' is simply the Old English 'blithe': joyful, cheerful, gay (in its original usage). 'Bosky' derives from *boscus*, Latin for bush, via the Middle English *busk* and *busch* (also meaning bush). So in its usual meaning bosky is 'bushy – a thicket'. It does, however appear in William Cope's *Glossary of Hampshire Words and Phrases* (1883) as 'elated with liquor', which leads me to conclude that the good physician was a Hampshire man.

His use of *borajo*, Old Spanish for 'drunk' (the contemporary Spanish is *borracho*) to describe the extreme stage of intoxication is inexplicable. In truth, polite Spanish has only a handful of words to describe intoxication. Italian and Greek have even fewer, and I read in a learned Canadian journal, the name of which escapes me, that Yiddish has only one. The article in question was in praise of Latin and Jewish moderation. The Scots tongue, by contrast, has dozens, and it is instructive to translate Mr Stewart's 'Three Stages' into demotic contemporary Scots.

In Scots, the 'Blythe' period would usually be referred to as 'fu', where the drinker is seen as a container of finite capacity beyond which the contents are likely to spill. This is similar to the English expression 'tanked up'. Equally widespread is 'bevvied', which is what happens when you consume lots of 'bevvy' (i.e. beverage), but also a corruption of the old French *beuvrage* (drink) and a reminder of *La Vieille Alliance*.

'Pished' is another familiar descriptive term for the first level of euphoria, perhaps describing the diuretic effect of alcohol. In spite of the enormous Scottish influence in the US, Americans look at you strangely if you use the word as a synonym for 'mildly drunk', since 'pissed' means irritated (i.e.'pissed off') in America.

Some parts of Scotland vary 'pished' with 'bladdered', or 'pure bladdered', but this is not to be confused with the more common expression, 'blootered', its diminutive 'plootered', or its extreme 'a mental blooter', all of which come from football: to blooter is to 'kick hard', as in 'blooter yir windae in wi the baw'.[1] The words are applied to excess generally, however, and particularly in relation to the consumption of alcohol.

'Miraculous' (pronounced in Glasgow 'marockyoolus' and sometimes abbreviated to 'maroc' or 'pure maroc') is a joyful description of the blythe state of mind, as is 'puggled' or 'half-puggled', which is usually applied to a 'foolish, clumsy or giggly' condition. The latter descriptors derive from the colourful term 'fu as a puggie' – 'puggie' being Scots for a piggie bank, a jackpot or a pool in cards. It is also a monkey, though this begs the question why poor monkeys should be considered 'fu'.

Then there is 'steamin', also 'steamboats' (as in 'he wuz steamboats'), perhaps a reference to the increased body heat referred to by Mr Stewart, although a recent article in *The Scotsman* made a connection between this usage and the immemorial custom of Clyde steamers opening their bars as soon as they put to sea. In turn, 'steamboats' gives rise to a 'steamer' (i.e. a drinking bout) and 'reekin', or the more oblique 'lummed up' ('lum' being a chimney or funnel, which 'reeks', steams or smokes).

'Fleein' (i.e. 'flying') is clearly within the happy or lively stage, as is 'hauf-scooped' (curiously, the term 'scooped', as in 'fully scooped', is unknown), while 'stottin' (pronounced *stoatin*: staggering; literally 'bouncing' or 'reeling') and its interesting derivative 'stotious' (pronounced *stoshus*) indicate a transition to the bosky condition.

Here we encounter a clutch of expressions which graphically depict the reveller as 'birlin' (spinning), 'wellied' (the reference here is to Wellington boots, now difficult to walk in, possibly owing to an accident connected to the aforementioned diuretic properties of alcohol) or 'skooshed'. The last seems to have joined the lexicon when lemonade or soda water became popular mixers; 'skoosh' is a Scots term for both. An earlier term is 'skelped' – a 'skelp' is a sharp blow to the side of the head ('just you shut yer mooth, or I'll gie yoos a skelp') and derives from the Gaelic *sgailc*, a morning dram. 'A man of the Hebrides,' wrote Dr Johnson, 'as soon as he appears in the morning swallows a glass of whisky; yet they are not a drunken race, at least I never was present at much intemperance; but no man is so abstemious as to refuse the morning dram, which they call a *skalk*.'

Then there is a clutch of words which graphically describe a condition of being out of control: 'destroyed', 'smashed', 'banjaxed' (this is Irish in origin; *Chambers Dictionary* suggests it is an elision of 'bang' and 'smashed'), 'bazooka'd', 'blitzed', 'numb', 'wastit' – or just plain 'ridiculous'.

'Guttered', a jocular reference to falling down in or having to crawl home via the gutter, may be seen as the transition to the final, borajo stage of drunkenness. Now the drinker is 'paralytic' (pronounced *paralettic* in Glasgow) or 'legless', an incapable, falling-down condition;[2] 'mortal', as in 'mortally pished' (also 'mortalled'; surely a reference to 'mortally wounded'); 'gutted' (evacuated, like a gutted fish), 'oot the box' or simply 'oot o' it' (it is debated whether 'box' here is 'brain' or 'coffin' – a related synonym is 'cased'). He may even 'take a whitey' (go deathly pale, prior to vomiting... or worse).

We may smile at such colourful descriptions, but I need hardly remind you, Dear Reader, that the three stages of intoxication are in direct correlation to the three phases of hangover: firstly, 'Fragile'; secondly, 'Very ill' and thirdly, 'Half dead'.

As ye sew, so shall ye reap!

This essay was first delivered to the Speculative Society, March 1998

---

[1] Stephen Mulrine, *The Coming of the Wee Malkies* (1937), included in *Voices of Our Time*, Ed. Maurice Lindsay (Edinburgh, 1971)

[2] On the west coast of Scotland it is maintained that the expression 'Legless in Glesga' inspired the title of Aldous Huxley's well-known book *Eyeless in Gaza* (1936), rather than John Milton's work of the same name. It is not known whether Milton ever visited Glasgow.

A drunken Tam O'Shanter, as portrayed in Robert Burns' poem of 1790, escapes the witches by crossing the Brig O'Doon on his horse Meg

THE CLASSIFICATION OF MALT WHISKIES

This blender's list from September 1974 demonstrates how malt and grain whiskies were considered from a blending perspective. The spellings have been left per the original list. All bear the names of the distilleries which made them, except the following:

Glen Craig was made at Glenburgie Distillery (1958–81), Mosstowie at Miltonduff Distillery (1956–81) and Lomond at Dumbarton Distillery (1959–91), all on Lomond stills.

Inverleven was a malt distillery within Dumbarton (grain whisky) Distillery (1959–91). Killyloch was within Moffat (grain whisky) Distillery (1965–85) and Kinclaith within Strathclyde (grain whisky) Distillery (1958–77).

Dumbuck and Dunglass were short-lived (1967) experimental malts, the former heavily peated, the latter with no peating, from Littlemill Distillery.

Ledaig is still being made at Tobermory Distillery, Inchmurrin and Rosdhu at Loch Lomond Distillery.

Glenisla-Glenlivet was an old name for Strathmill Distillery.

Observations

- All the top-class malts are Speysides.

- All the second-class malts are Speysides, apart from Highland Park, Talisker and (Royal) Lochnagar.

- The only Speyside malt to have disappeared since 1974 is Parkmore (distillery closed 1988); the make from the three other Speyside distilleries which have closed since 1974 (Dallas Dhu, Coleburn and Pittyvaich) is still available, although rare in the case of the first two.

- Since 1974, the axe has fallen on distilleries producing second- and third-class Highland malts and in the Lowlands.

- Although their malts were still available in 1974, four of the latter closed in the 1920s, as did Glencawdor (Nairn) and Towiemore (Botriphnie, Banff). Glenfyne (Ardrishaig) closed in 1937 and Strathdee (Aberdeen) in 1938.

- Seventeen Campbeltown distilleries also closed between 1920 and 1934, yet the only whiskies available to blenders in 1974 were from the two distilleries operating today.

- See page 276 for a complete list of distillery openings and closures since 1900.

HIGHLANDS

TOP CLASS

Aultmore	Glen Elgin	Glenlossie	Longmorn
Benrinnes	Glen Grant	Glenrothes	Macallan
Cragganmore	Glenlivet	Linkwood	Mortlach

1ST CLASS

Balmenach	Craigellachie	Glenfiddich	Mosstowie
Balvenie	Dailuaine	Glen Keith	Strathisla
Benriach	Glenburgie	Highland Park	Talisker
Caperdonich	Glendronach	Lochnagar	Tomintoul
Cardow	Glenfarclas	Milton Duff	

2ND CLASS

Aberfeldy	Dalmore	Glenmorangie	Ord
Aberlour	Dalwhinnie	Glen Moray	Parkmore★
Ardmore	Deanston	Glenspey	Pulteney
Banff★	Dufftown	Glentauchers	Rosdhu
Blair Athol	Glenallachie	Glenury★	Speyburn
Brackla	Glencadam★	Knockando	Strathmill
Clynelish	Glen Craig★	Knockdhu	Tamdhu
Coleburn★	Glendullan	Macduff★	Teaninich
Convalmore★	Glenfyne★	Millburn★	Tormore
Dallas Dhu★	Glenglassaugh★	Oban	

3RD CLASS

Allt a' Bhainne	Dunglass★	Glen Ugie★	Scapa
Balblair	Edradour	Imperial★	Speyside
Ben Nevis	Fettercairn	Inchgower	Strathdee★
Ben Wyvis★	Glen Albyn	Inchmurrin	Strathmore★
Benromach	Glencawdor★	Killyloch★	Tamnavulin
Braes of	Glengarioch	Ledaig	Tomatin
Glenlivet	Glenlochy★	Lochside★	Towiemore★
Brechin★	Glen Mhor★	Lomond★	Tullibardine
Dumbuck★	Glen Turret	North Port★	

LOWLANDS

Auchentoshan
Auchtermuchty★
Auchtertool★
Bankier★
Bladnoch
Glengoyne

Glenkinchie
Inverleven★
Kinclaith★
Ladyburn★
Linlithgow★
Littlemill★

Provanmill★
Rosebank★

GRAIN WHISKIES

Ben Nevis★
Caledonian★
Cambus★
Cameronbridge
Carsebridge★
Dumbarton★

Garnheath★
Girvan
Invergordon
Lochside★
Montrose★
North British

North of Scotland★
Port Dundas
Strathclyde

ISLAYS

Ardbeg
Bowmore
Bruichladdich
Bunnahabhain

Caol Ila
Glenisla★
Jura
Lagavulin

Laphroaig
Port Ellen★

CAMPBELTOWNS

Glen Scotia

Springbank

★ = *distillery closed*

GRAIN DISTILLERIES 1900 TO PRESENT
14 distilleries closed, 10 distilleries opened (7 of them now closed)

CLOSURES
Adelphi (1851–1902)
Dundashill (1899–1903)
Saucel (1855–1903, but malt
   distilling continued until 1915)
Ardgowan (1896–1907)
Camlachie (1834–1920)
Gartloch (1897–1921)
Bo'ness (1876–1925)
Yoker (1845–1927)
Montrose★ (1934–1964)
Strathmore (1957–1982)
Carsebridge (1852–1983; founded
   1799 as a malt distillery)
Caledonian (1855–1987)
Cambus (1806– 1993)

OPENINGS
Strathclyde (1927–)
Dumbarton (1938–2003)
Strathmore (1957–1982)
Invergordon (1959–)
Girvan (1963–)
Moffat (1965–1985)
Montrose★ (1934–1964)

★Montrose, aka Hillside or
Glenesk, was founded 1897,
converted to grain whisky
production in 1934, and
reverted to malt whisky
production 1964–1985

GRAIN DISTILLERIES CURRENTLY IN OPERATION
★Cameronbridge, Fife
Girvan, Ayrshire
Invergordon, Ross & Cromarty

★North British, Edinburgh
★Port Dundas, Glasgow
Strathclyde, Glasgow
★ *These founded pre-1900*

MALT DISTILLERIES 1900 TO PRESENT
C = Campbeltown; S = Speyside

1900–1920
14 distilleries closed 1 distillery opened

CLOSURES
Drumcaldie (1896–1903)
Ardgowan (1896–1908)
Nevis (1878–1908)
Bon Accord (1855–1910)
Grandtully (1825–1910)
Tambowie (1825–1910)
Auchnagie (1833–1911)
Benachie (1824–1915)

Devanha (1825–1915)
Glenaden (1882–1915)
Glentarras (1852–1915)
Greenock (1795–1915)
Langholm (1765–1915)
Clydesdale (1825–1919)

OPENINGS
Malt Mill (1908–1960,
   within Lagavulin Distillery)

1920–1930
38 distilleries closed; no new distilleries

Camlachie, (1834-1920)
Kirkliston (1795-1920)
Annandale (1830-1920/21)
Dalaruan (C) (1825-1922)
Dean (1881-1922)
Provanmill (1815-1922)
Ardlussa (C) (1879-1923)
Argyll (C) (1844-1923)
Kintyre (C) (1825-1923)
Glenfoyle (1826-1923)
Glen Nevis (C) (1877-1923)
Burnside (C) (1825-1924)
Campbeltown (C) (1817-1924)
Dalintober (1832-1925)
Edinburgh, Sciennes (1849-1925)
Glengyle (C) (1873-1925)
Grange, Burntisland (1786-1925)
Hazelburn (C) (1796-1925)
Lochruan (C) (1835-1925)
Auchinblae (1896-1926)
Auchtermuchty (1829-1926)
Ben Wyvis (1879-1926)

Glenside (C) (1830-1926)
Glenskiach (1896-1926)
Isla (1851-1926)
Kinloch (C)(1823-1926)
Springside (C) (1830-1926)
Albyn (C)(1830-1927)
Auchtertool (1845-1927)
Ballechin (1810-1927)
Benmore (C)(1868-1927)
Glencawdor (1898-1927)
Bankier (1828-1928)
Lochhead (C) (1824-1928)
Stromness (1817-1928)
Stronachie (1900-1928)
Lochindaal (1829-1929)
Glencoull (1897-1929)

1930–1960
5 distilleries closed, 7 new distilleries

CLOSURES

Towiemore (1896-1930)
Parkmore (S) (1894-1931)
Riechlachan (C) (1825-1934)
Glenfyne (1831-1937)
Strathdee (1821-1938)

OPENINGS

Inverleven (1938-1991, within Dumbarton Distillery)
Tullibardine (1949-)
Speyside (S) (1955-)
Glen Keith (S) (1957-)
Kinclaith (1957/58-1976, within Strathclyde Distillery)
Lochside (1957-1984)
Tormore (S) (1958-)

1960–1980
3 distilleries closed, 16 new distilleries

CLOSURES

Ladyburn (1966-1975, within
  Girvan Distillery)
Kinclaith (1957/58-1976)
Ben Wyvis (1965-1977, within
  Invergordon Distillery

OPENINGS

Macduff (1962-)
Tomintoul (S) (1964-)
Ben Wyvis (1965-1977)
Deanston (1965-)
Glen Flagler (1965-1985, within
  Moffat Distillery)

Killyloch (1965-1985, within
  Moffat Distillery)
Lochlomond (1965-)
Tamnavulin (1965-)
Ladyburn (1966-1975)
Clynelish II (1967-)
Glenallachie (S) (1967-)
Mannochmore (S) (1971-)
Braes of Glenlivet (S) (1973-)
Auchroisk (S)(1974-)
Allt a'Bhainne (S) (1975-)
Pittyvaich (S) (1975-1993)

1980–PRESENT
22 distilleries closed, 7 new distilleries

CLOSURES

Dallas Dhu (S) (1899-1983)
Glen Albyn (1846-1983)
Glenlochy (1898-1983)
Glen Mhor (1892-1983)
Glenugie (1831-1983)
North Port (1820-1983)
Port Ellen (1825-1983)
St Magdalene, Linlithgow
  (1798-1983)
Lochside, Montrose (1957-1984)
Coleburn (S) (1897-1985)
Convalmore (S) (1894-1985)
Killyloch (1965-1985)
Glenesk, Hillside (1897-1985)
Glen Flagler (1965-1985)
Glenury Royal (1825-1985)

Millburn (1807-1985)
Glenglassaugh (1875-1986)
Inverleven (1938-1991)
Lomond (1959-1991)
Pittyvaich (S) (1975-1993)
Rosebank (1840-1993)
Littlemill (1772-1994)

OPENINGS

Kininvie (S) (1990-, within
  Glenfiddich Distillery)
Isle of Arran (1995-)
Glengyle (2004-)
Kilchoman (2005-)
Ladybank (proposed)
Blackford (proposed)
Daftmill (2005-)
Barra (proposed 2004)

INDEX